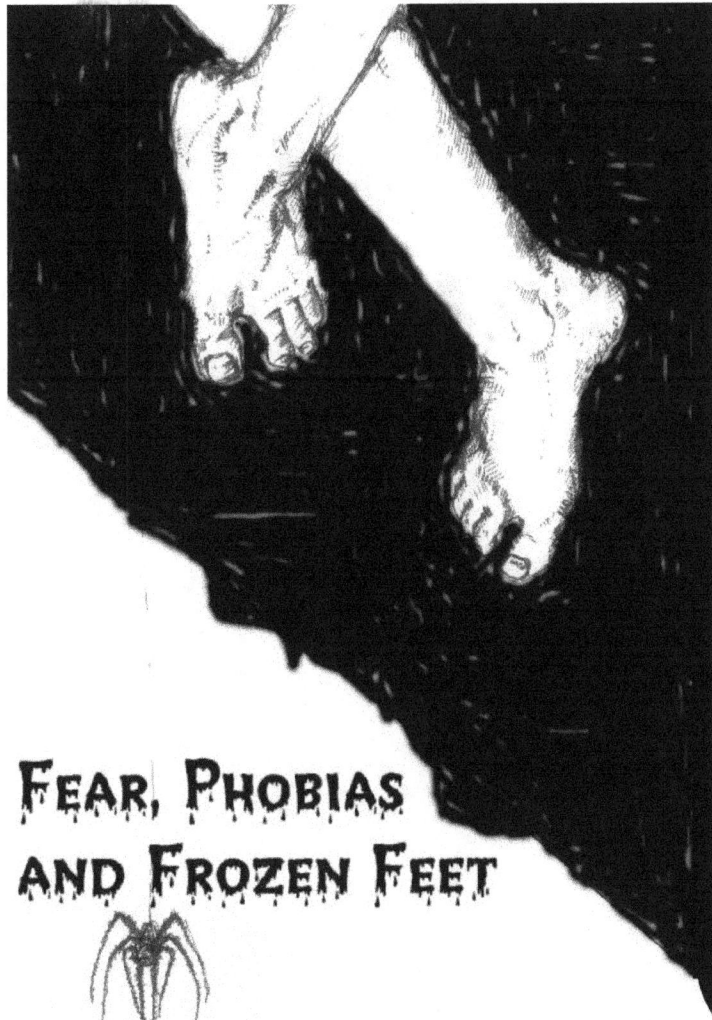

# Fear, Phobias and Frozen Feet

## Cindy van den Heuvel

# Fear, Phobias and Frozen Feet

By

**Cindy van den Heuvel**

*This book is dedicated to my wonderful children who have stood by me through thick and thin, occasionally helped me to defeat dragons, slay vampires and fend off other unsavory characters.*

# ACKNOWLEDGEMENTS

Many people, often unwittingly, help when writing a book such as this.

Thanks to all the people to whom I chatted on the internet in various chatrooms, for your advice, shared life experiences and support while I was doing my research for this book.

Thanks to my Mum who has always been my secret supporter.

Thanks to my late grandmother, Winifred Vine and late Aunt Joy Phillips, who inspired me, were my role-models and encouraged me to have a positive attitude in life.

Thanks also to the first ex-wife, Cinzia Busi, my friends the Stevensons, Glynnis Georgeu and Diana Turner - for their critique.

A special thanks to Rob Stark – my longtime friend and editor.

Thanks Guys, you're all great!

Cindy

# CONTENTS

# INTRODUCTION

In my line of work I get to meet a lot of people. People are definitely one of the most fascinating creatures ever created. Many of us never seem to learn from our mistakes, and sooner or later find ourselves repeating the same bad patterns and habits over and over again, rather like a stuck record. (Not that many people even know what records are anymore!)

After finding myself in yet another situation, and yet another drama, I began to think, hey, maybe this isn't just my bad luck. Maybe I don't wear a sign saying DUMB GULLIBLE BASTARD on my forehead. Maybe this is just me and what I am and nothing to do with other people. So I then embarked on a journey of reflection, and when I started talking to other people about my problem of always entering into relationships with the same kind of people, no matter where in the world I was, I made the astounding discovery that I was not alone! I didn't have DUMB GULLIBLE BASTARD tattooed on my forehead! Can you believe, there are many other incredibly bright, intelligent, caring people out there playing the same dumb game. My first thought was, as this game is such a popular sport, maybe we can get it into the next Olympics, but then I realised, no city on this planet would be big enough to host all the competitors.

So, if you are a champion player in this game, or know of someone who is – then please read this book or pass this book onto them. Because, this book isn't about playing the game, as we all know how to do that already, it's about changing the rules!

In researching this book, I came across an outstanding psychological principle called the Drama Triangle. This was first identified by Stephen Karpman in 1968, and is used by many psychotherapists today. Understanding and just knowing about the games we play in the drama triangle, has changed my life completely. I can stop myself before going into one of the three roles he identified - the Victim, Persecutor and Rescuer. It's like the awareness of this triangle has put an alarm in my head. It goes off "...beep barp beep barp..." Whenever I start slipping into the familiar roles I used to play in this game. I can now take a step back and say to myself, "Hold on here, if you do this then you are going to end up as a rescuer again!" What we all need to be aware of, is that there are no winners in this game. Another interesting fact, is that it's our fears that drive us to play these games. Most of us react the way we do because of some or other subconscious fear. Often, we don't even know that we have these fears, but they rule us completely. What are your fears, what fears drive you?

The stories in this book are all true or based on true events and real people. However, I felt it best to change names and little personal details, as I don't want to piss people off that they come harassing me. I'm sure you understand, it's not that I'm paranoid or something, but...**HEY! WHAT THE HELL ARE YOU LOOKING AT?**

**Ablutophobia- Fear of washing or bathing.**

# CHAPTER 1
## When your arse is at your side and not on your butt.

Jason held his glass in the air, seemingly to stare at the colour of the beer inside. The other couples around the table all waited expectantly for his comment, as one could tell by his intense expression, that a really good life insight was on its way. "I am the kind of man," he said at last with great gravity, "that doesn't judge a book by its cover. I look at what's inside, I'm not concerned about outer appearances." He paused while he looked around the table at the other couples. Jason had great public speaking skills and the knack of being able to control a large audience. The Bowling Club in Francistown, Botswana, was the usual place for most ex-pats to hang out during the day on the weekend. And since we joined, Jason had managed to always draw a big crowd around him during drink breaks. As they had only known him for a month, they still thought he was fantastic. Of course, after 9 years of being with him I knew my place and that it was not required of me to talk or show anybody that I might have a brain. All I was required to do, was sit there dumbly and smile adoringly at him, like some love-sick cow. Jason took a sip of his beer, pursed his lips so that they looked like a chicken's bum, and said something that'll haunt me for the rest of my life. "Look at my wife Katy sitting over there. She's living proof of what I'm trying to say. If I was only concerned about the outward appearance of people, I'd never be seen dead with a dog like Katy." All eyes around the table swiveled to look at me. I could feel the heat rush up and my face turn bright red with embarrassment. Although it was 48 degrees outside, I knew it was not the temperature that made my face feel so hot. I suddenly had the desire to start barking, or maybe howling like a dog hit by a truck. After all, he did just refer to me as a dog. But, I remained subdued, smiling idiotically, all the while dying a slow death inside. However, he wasn't yet finished with his words of wisdom, he had more knowledge to impart. "You see, let me tell you something about Katy. Although she has no looks, and most men wouldn't be seen dead with her…" I had a quick look around the table and noticed that many people were starting to look uncomfortable and embarrassed, some were wriggling a little in their seats. "…Katy has a heart of gold and will do anything to help people. That's why I am with her, not because of her dog looks, but because of her good heart. I look at what's inside, not on what's outside." He finished this comment off with a smug smile, quickly downed the rest of the beer in his glass and stood up, ready to go back to the greens. Everybody at the table looked shocked and avoided looking me in the eye. I just smiled, as I was used to Jason putting me down in public. It gave him a feeling of power and control, but this time I think he went a bit too far. From that moment on, people avoided us at the club, we became social lepers. But I

4

Turn me back!
I promise not
to behave like
an arse again!

was used to that, as that usually happened after people knew Jason for about a month or so. However, on this specific occasion, I decided that I wasn't going to let Jason get away with it yet again, so when we got home, I confronted him. "How could you say that about me at the club, how could you call me a dog in front of all those people?" I could feel tears of indignation filling my eyes, but I vowed that I wouldn't give him the pleasure of seeing me cry.

As he looked at me, a dark cloud seemed to move across his face, and his face became grotesque as it did whenever I made him angry, which was quite often. His eyes changed from amber to black and he spat out in fury, "You ungrateful bitch! Can't you even take a compliment! I was just complimenting you in front of those people, but no, nobody dare ever compliment you!" He flung his dinner plate onto the floor, breaking it into a myriad of pieces. It was left to me to grovel on the floor to clean up the mess.

You might ask, why did I put up with his bad behaviour? When I met him, I was outgoing and vivacious and was quite the social creature. Jason appeared to be strong and someone who could look after me. I had decided at about the time I met Jason, that I wanted to have a family, a providing husband and a house with a white picket fence – the fifties dream, but in the late 80s! I was tired of being independent and having to make all my decisions in my life. I wanted someone who could take care of me. Within a few days of moving in with Jason, I realised that he was a lie. Everything about him was a lie, most of what he said was a lie, and the tragedy was, he didn't believe they were lies. I soon came to see that if he couldn't cope with reality, he would just invent a new reality and as his partner, I'd have to go along with him to save face and live his lie with him. As soon as I rebelled, I would be put down in public and back into my place, under his feet as his personal doormat, where he could wipe the dog doo off his shoes. I changed from having an outgoing personality, someone who was never afraid to speak her mind, into a timid little mouse. My friends and family were horrified in the change in me, and they all hated Jason as a result. I sprang to his defence time and time again, he had had a hard life, his ex-wife was mean to him, every boss he had was mean to him that's why he couldn't hold down a job. So in the 10 years we were together, he only ever contributed to the family income for 2 of them.

So, why did I stick with him? I wanted the dream
so badly I was prepared to sacrifice me. Jason kept
me there at the end of his leash by making me believe
that I was so worthless and so useless no man would
ever want me, and he was doing me an almighty
favour by keeping me there. If I left him I'd never
have another man again, and I was scared of being
alone. Jason played on my fear of being alone and
unwanted. As time went by, I started standing up
more and more for myself and deliberately doing
things which I knew would irritate him. Like chatting
to a friend I met at the local supermarket. Jason would
time me whenever I went to the supermarket, or
anywhere for that matter. He would work out how
long it should take me, and if I was late (in his mind)
he would be pacing up and down the deck when I got
back. He would get angry and shout and yell and
threaten to kill us all. He never allowed time for me to
chat to someone in the supermarket, so I would go out
of my way to chat to people, just to make me a little
late. (I suppose I was mean, but it was fun at the
time.) I think living in a relationship that was so out
of whack and so out of control, that little action of
mine gave me some control. Well, at least in my mind
it did.

Over the years I had gone over the edge from time
to time and thrown him out, but he always threatened
suicide, so I let him back. After 10 years he started
threatening to kill all of us, not just himself, and I sold
all our furniture in one day while he was out, and fled
up north under assumed names. Finally I managed to
escape with the children, and did he kill himself? Not

likely. In less than a year after our divorce he married a woman 17 years his senior. She turned into an alcoholic after he beat her up physically and put her in hospital, then he moved onto someone else, then she dumped him, now he's with someone else. The last I heard he sent me an email saying he had finally hooked the right one who could take care of him as she had a good job. Well, good luck to him. He's never ever paid child support for his children.

It's amazing when you talk to people, male and female, how many go through similar experiences to the ones I've just mentioned. We are good people, right? So, why do we end up with real arseholes? We know how to choose our friends and we know how to be selective when we take on new jobs, so why don't we know how to choose partners? Is it love that really blinds us to their true colours, or do they hide them from us until they have us hooked? Or do we perhaps look on them as a challenge, as something we can change or mould? What I don't understand, is how everybody else, family and friends, and sometimes total strangers, can immediately sense them for what they are, but we live with them and are completely unaware – or are we?

I just remember every time somebody said something negative about Jason to me, I would immediately leap to his defence, make excuses for him, feel slighted and do all I could to protect him. I lost close friends as a result of doing just that, and distanced myself from my family, as they just didn't understand him. Now I look back and realise how right they were, what good caring people they were just looking out for me, and I feel like a fool for not believing them. Sometimes, more often than not, family and friends are exactly on the mark. They know you better than you know yourself and it hurts them to see you being badly treated or dragged down by the one you're with.

You could end up with a partner that looks good, but comes with a heap of problems that drag you down. For some strange reason these people, the energy sappers I call them, very seldom rise up to your level, but drag you down to theirs. They wear you out, feeding off your energy so they stay strong and you get weaker and weaker until you're bashed, battered emotionally and crushed. When they have no more use for you, or you can't take it anymore, the relationship ends, you recover slowly and the next day they're already with a new partner.

This is an amazing game we play, called the Rescuer, Persecutor and Victim game. You start out as the Rescuer and end up as the Victim, while the original Victim heads off to find a new Rescuer. Or sometimes, you can move from Victim to Rescuer and then on to Persecutor. Sometimes, when you are the Victim, you want nobody to rescue you and you hop out of the game for a while, so over time you build yourself up to a position of strength again, as that's what you do as that's your personality. You are the ultimate survivor in the ultimate real-life reality show.

James had an anger management problem. When things didn't go his own way, he would punch the wall

and break things, rather like a two year old having a
tantrum. This scared Mandy quite a bit, and she went
out of her way to keep James calm, and reduce his
anger. However, over the months, he started pushing
and shoving her as well. He never punched her, but
pushed her hard enough into walls to give her bruises.
James blamed Mandy for everything that went wrong,
and justified his breaking things in anger, by saying,
"Well, at least I didn't hit you!" James was the
Persecutor in this game, refusing to take responsibility
for his own actions, and blaming others. Mandy, was
the victim. When James progressed to pushing and
shoving Mandy into the wall, she would cry out in
pain, and James would collapse on the floor and cry
like a baby, apologising over and over again for what
he had done. Mandy would put aside her own pain,
and comfort James and tell him that everything was all
right. This is a role reversal, Mandy is now a Rescuer
and James is a Victim. They would swap roles once
more, with James changing into a Rescuer, to cook
Mandy dinner, bring her breakfast in bed and give her
footrubs. Mandy, would become the persecutor,
giving him the silent treatment and sighing every time
he came near her. This sort of pattern happens in
many relationships, when the one partner can't handle
stress, often the stress of their job or family life, and
they take their frustrations out on their partner.

David was always a little moody when he and Jenna
were dating. Sometimes he would take off for no
reason and not say where he was going. Most times
he only ever talked about himself or his job. He
showed Jenna very little affection, but when he did,

she felt that it made up for his moodiness. David was an absolute hunk, and all Jenna's friends were envious that she had managed to snag him. Jenna truly believed, that if she loved David enough, she could change him, and stop him from being verbally abusive and cold towards her. They went for counselling, and David confessed that he only became distant and angry with Jenna when he didn't have sex often enough. Jenna said that she didn't feel like having sex with David when he was moody.

The two of them are taking turns to play the persecutor and victim role in their relationship, and because of their fears, they aren't communicating their needs to each other at all.

Greg thought that Samantha was the girl of his dreams. That was, until he found out that she had been cheating on him with his best friend. He was devastated and ended the relationship with both Samantha, and his best friend. Samantha soon dumped his best friend, and started seeing someone else. Greg took some time out from relationships, to take stock of his life. He met an awesome girl at work, and started seeing her. Greg though that things could get quite serious with his new partner. Somehow or other, Samantha found out about Greg's new love. She went into mourning, lost weight and stopped looking after herself. Samantha started stalking Greg, and following him wherever he went. He would wake up in the morning, to find her sitting in her car parked in his drive. Greg felt incredibly guilty about the obvious torment Samantha was going through, and started phoning her again and occasionally taking her out for dinner, to make her feel better and ease his guilt. Of course, his new partner didn't like that when she found out about it, so she dumped him. Greg had moved from Victim to Rescuer and back to Victim. On the other hand, Samantha had moved from Persecutor to Victim and back to Persecutor. When Greg's new relationship ended, Samantha told Greg that he was boring; that was why nobody wanted him, and then she just disappeared out of his life. Greg was left wondering what he had done wrong.

People do truly awful things to each other in relationships. Megan was attracted to Craig's intellect and dry sense of humour. Megan says, "I lost 'me' in doing whatever he wanted to make him happy. But he was never happy, no matter what I did." Megan stopped being with her friends, stopped going shopping, stopped going out to lunch, so she could be available whenever Craig needed her. She ran herself ragged, working long hours every day, so she could earn extra money to buy the things he wanted. Craig complained about everything she did and complained constantly about the state the house was in. Megan would work, cleaning the house until the early hours, to have the house looking just the way he wanted. But Craig still wasn't happy. He would go out drinking every night after work, and blame that on Megan as her constant house-cleaning got on his nerves. Megan ate alone most nights. Weekends would come along and they would be invited out to BBQs. Then Craig would complain about what a mess the house was in, so Megan would have to stay at home all weekend cleaning the house, while Craig went out with his friends. The more Megan tried to make Craig happy, the more power and control it gave him. Craig was stuck in the Persecutor role, as many control-freaks are. There was no way that Megan was going to change his behaviours, as he was always right. Or was he?

Many times, we fall in love with the 'idea' of the person, a fantasy that is backed by the things they promised. We get confused and anxious when their actions contradict this fantasy image we have in our minds. Out of the fear we feel when we are confused, we react and say things, often slipping into the Persecutor role. Our partner is not prepared to take responsibility for anything they've done, and accuse you straight back. This often sets up a war-zone in the home, with each partner constantly sniping at the other, and reading negative insights into everything the other one says. So if you say, "Your hair looks nice today," they react with some cutting comment, believing that you obviously don't think that their hair looked nice on other days. Which, as we know, was definitely not what you meant at all.

The good news is that it is possible to leave this game. The how I shall tell you about later. The important thing to remember, is that inside, the manipulator, the serial bully, the control-freak, the abuser, the player, the serial cheater, the joker who can never be serious for half a minute, the nagger, the whiner, the addict and the many other kinds of people who hold you back in a relationship, deep inside, it is their fears which are causing them to behave in this way. It is nothing you are doing or have done, it is their problem - not yours.

How do I know if I am in an abusive relationship?

There are many different kinds of abuse, some subtle and some not so subtle. It's the not so subtle kinds of abuse that we are most familiar with and more easily able to identify. We have seen the movies, where Jennifer Lopez gets beaten black and blue in 'Enough' and heard people verbally abusing others around us. The signs of that kind of abuse is so obvious, we can't miss it, and we feel sorry for those people who have to put up with it. However, it's the subtle kinds of abuse that is far more damaging. Many of us face it every day - by our children, partners, bosses, people at work, and we don't even realise it is happening to us until it is too late and our self-esteem has taken a large knock. Remember, nothing but nothing excuses selfish, disrespectful behaviour towards another human being. To show disrespect for another is to show disrespect for one's self.
So, what exactly is abuse and how do we know we are being abused?
It doesn't matter whether you are being physically, emotionally or verbally abused, the bottom line is that abuse is always about control. It is about one partner using strategies and techniques to control the other. It is about your partner's behaviours changing your personality, and you losing your self-esteem and your

14

feeling of self-worth.  It is about someone using your fears to manipulate you to do what they want and be what they want.  They make you afraid to be yourself, afraid to control yourself, so therefore you will be available to be controlled by them.

Some red flags to look out for.

If you are faced with any of these red flags, you could be in an abusive relationship of some kind.  I am not going to list the obvious signs of abuse as we're all familiar with those already.

1.  Your partner controls your time by making you wait - it could be waiting for them to do something after they've watched just one more TV programme or played just one more game, or even by not giving you a direct answer to your question and replying with a "We'll have to wait and see" or "We'll talk about it later", and later never comes.  If the person who has to wait complains, they are criticised for not having enough patience, or of trying to start a fight.  Either way, they are being manipulated.  This type of control is two-fold:  Their time is controlled and then they are blamed for it!

2.  Your partner controls your time by timing you whenever you go out somewhere without them.  If you take longer than they mentally calculated you'd take, they lay a guilt trip on you to make you feel bad.

3.  Your partner withholds information from you, and you either have to beg for it, or are forced to try and act on your own.  This means that you'll either take longer or will have a greater chance of failure.  This form of control makes the abuser feel superior as they know more than you do.

15

4. Your partner withholds needed money, and you are forced to beg, plead or do without. The situation is then turned around that it was your 'trying to be a martyr' or your begging which forced them to withhold the money.

5. Your partner controls all the finances, gives you an allowance that isn't enough and deprives you of necessities, while they buy whatever they want and spend money like there's no tomorrow. They don't ask your permission before they buy something, but because they control your finances, you have to ask their permission if you want to buy something.

6. Your partner controls your emotions by using body language and gestures. These can be - sulking, giving you the silent treatment, turning their back on you and walking away while you're still talking to them, stomping out of the room and hitting or kicking something as they leave, rolling their eyes in disgust while you are talking or doing something, sighing deeply, refusing to look you in the eye, making a big show of crossing their arms with a bored look on their faces, withholding affection or sex, ignoring you in company and talking animatedly to others.

7. Your partner controls you by defining your reality. They discount your experiences and replace it with their truth and reality which is actually a lie. For example, "That's not what happened," "That's not what I said," "That's not what you saw or felt," or the best one of all "I know you better than you know yourself!"

8. Your partner controls you by making you responsible for their behaviour, and in doing this

avoids all accountability. It will be your fault because you didn't remind them, or set a good example, or stop them soon enough when you saw they were doing the wrong thing. You might ask your partner for their input, they reply, "Whatever," and then when you go ahead and do it, it's all your fault if it doesn't work.

9. Your partner controls you by putting you down all the time, in public and in private. They play down your successes and talents, belittle you and then praise you for trivial things you do, thus saying that you are best suited for doing trivial things. They might make offensive jokes about you in public, mimic you, laugh or smirk at you, patronise you, insult you or make rude sounds while you talk.

10. Your partner controls you by talking about you in company in front of you as if you weren't there. They can bring up private moments that you might not want to be general knowledge, and turn it around so that you come out as the fool and they come out as the hero. This way they can make you the brunt of jokes and a laughing stock among your friends.

A healthy relationship is a partnership and consists of giving and taking. Each partner knows that sacrifices and concessions they make will eventually be returned. They are also able to accept themselves for who they are with all warts and imperfections, and also to accept their partner for who they are and with all their blemishes and imperfections. Unfortunately, an abusive relationship is one-sided. The abusive partner can't give and take, and takes any criticism personally as a personal assault on their character.

The abusive partner needs to win in order to feel in control. That's all that makes them feel okay and there is intense pressure for them to hold onto control and thereby preserve that 'winning feeling'. It is unacceptable and never crosses their minds to be wrong, give in, or place another's needs above their own. The terrible reality, is that you can't change an abusive partner. I once thought, if I loved Jason enough I could change him, but I was wrong. You can't change another person, unless you use abusive tactics. Change has to come from within.

So, you've just met the partner of your dreams. You are still in the 'honeymoon' phase of your relationship. You both bend over backwards to accommodate each other's needs and wants, as your partner being happy is your number one aim. What red flags could you start looking out for, which could indicate your partner's true personality once the 'honeymoon' is over?

Watch out for these red flags!
1. How do they act with others? If they are nasty or disrespectful, or poke fun at them, chances are it could happen to you.
2. Do they drink too much? Is there a personality change when they are drunk? Do they become aggressive towards their friends?
3. Do they take drugs to help them 'relax'?
4. Do you feel stifled and that your 'space' is constantly being invaded?
5. Are they abusive?
6. Do they take pleasure in hurting animals?

7.  What kinds of relationships do they have with their immediate family?

8.  Do they respect the law or are they constantly looking for ways to take things to the max?

9.  Do they congratulate their friends on their infidelity?

10.  Are little things they're doing starting to worry you?

11.  Do you catch them out lying a lot?

12.  Do they think shoplifting is a challenge?

13.  Do they operate on a very short fuse?

14.  Do they break things when they get angry?

15.  Do they suffer from road rage and shout and swear at other drivers on the road?

16.  Are they always right no matter what?

17.  Is everything always everybody else's fault?

18.  Can they admit when they're wrong or make a mistake, and can they say sorry?

19.  Do your friends and family not like your new choice of partner, and keep warning you against them?

20.  Do you sometimes pretend not to be home or avoid their call when you see it's their number?

21.  Do they tell you you're fat, what to eat and what clothes to wear?

So either you or your partner has decided to pull the plug on your relationship.  As is natural, you are feeling pretty devastated.  Here are the Top 30 coping strategies when a relationship ends.

**Top 30 post-relationship coping strategies**

1.  When you can't stop thinking about an ex, try and change your thought patterns about them. Distract yourself with other things and thoughts. This isn't easy, it takes a concerted effort, time and hard work. Eventually you will look back on your memories without feeling any pain. The bad memories will subside, and the good memories will remain.

2.  Often, when a relationship ends, one partner still has strong feelings of love for the other. Don't concentrate on your feelings for your ex as you'll start to obsess and will have problems moving on. You lived, laughed and loved before you met your ex. You will live, laugh and love again. As humans, we're very resillient and time does heal as you adjust and learn to cope.

3.  Don't tell your ex about your thoughts, pain, feelings and hurts. You might find it soothing at the time, but it makes your ex think you're pathetic. If you're doing it to try and make them feel guilty, don't bother, because they won't. Rather write down all your thoughts, feelings, etc and put it somewhere safe in a drawer. This helps as you've got it all off your chest. Don't give in to the temptation to give your ex the letter. They are really not interested in what you have to say. They have moved on.

4.  The most important thing is to keep your mind occupied. Some people throw themselves into their job. Just think of all the extra money you can earn working overtime!

5.  Talk to friends and family when you're feeling down, or throw a pity party for yourself. But, don't go

on and on, as they'll soon tire of your misery and avoid you because they think you're hard work.

6.  Go out and do something you've always wanted to do, but never had the time to do. Don't have the money? Cut back on something else and splurge! Treat yourself; you deserve it.

7.  We can't change things others do. No amount of stress or worrying about things will change the situation. So, accept what's happened and move on. Dwelling on this and over-analysing everything will only hurt you more.

8.  When you become sad or miss your ex, remind yourself of how you felt whenever they intentionally did or said something to hurt you. You don't really want this person in your life. You deserve much better.

9.  If all else fails, don't feel too embarrassed to get professional help to help with the break-up.

10. Remember, that often it's not the actual person you miss, but the emotion that was created during the good times. You can recapture that same emotion again with someone else.

11. Keep reminding yourself on how important it is, to take care of you. Don't worry about the ex. How they cope with the break-up is not your problem, but their problem.

12. Take up an activity that your ex wouldn't have enjoyed, but you always wanted to do. This'll give you the opportunity to meet other people with similar interests to yourself.

13. Visit friends and family you haven't seen for ages.

14. Don't be tempted to visit your ex for one last farewell sex session. Your ex will just be using you. Dynamite sex won't change their mind and make them come running back to you, and you'll just feel empty and depressed afterwards.

15. Avoid a rebound relationship if you possibly can. You don't want to set up another Victim for hurt and pain. You need to work through your issues first, spend time with yourself and let yourself heal.

16. Write down goals for yourself. They can be small goals like, "Phone Mum once a week." Put them on your fridge. It helps to keep you on task, stay focused and gives you something to look forward to, which is very important at this time.

17. Take the opportunity to spring-clean your life and make changes. Look on the whole episode as a self-growing process.

18. The best revenge is to be happy. Find something to make you smile about at least once a day.

19. If the ex tells you they found someone better than you, don't dwell on it. It just tells you what a sorry character they have. Also, remember that many hurtful words are said during a break-up, which are regretted later. Take them from where they've come.

20. Go to a travel agent and look through travel brochures. Even if you don't have the money to travel at this stage, it could be a goal to focus on – saving money to travel. What this does do, is show you that there is a big wide world out there and there are many other experiences waiting for you to experience, apart from your ex.

21. Read all you can about divorce or ending relationships. It helps to know that there are others out there who have gone through what you're going through now and survived. It'll be very encouraging for you.

22. Go away for a weekend, take a friend with you, and explore some nearby town or village you've never been to before.

23. You will need all your reserves so pamper yourself as much as possible. Eat healthily; join a gym and work out to get rid of all the hurt and anger inside you.

24. Start thinking about your ex as a bad habit you need to break.

25. Don't try to find reasons why your relationship ended, why your ex didn't want you, lied to you, cheated on you or whatever. Because, the truth is, there is no one answer, no one reason. Dwelling on possible reasons, who's to blame, who did what and who said what, will get you nowhere fast. The fact is, obsessing about the *whys* and *hows* could actually make you physically ill. The ex has gone. The relationship is over and nothing you do or say will change that.

26. Don't try to force or manipulate someone to love you or be with you. You lose your self-respect if you do that, and they won't respect you if you try. Don't call them and then hang-up or start stalking them. It makes you come across as pathetic and desperate.

27. Easy to say I know, but accept what has happened to you. Find someone who makes you happier than your ex. The only person who can stop that from happening, is you.

28. If you try everything and still can't stop obsessing about your ex, then you might have been in an addictive relationship. Recognise that you are hooked and write down all the things that fed your addiction in the relationship. Now write down all the negative things and feelings you experienced in the relationship. For this to work you have to remove your rose-coloured glasses and be very honest. It's like a *Pros* and *Cons* list. Read through what you've written. No doubt, if you've been honest with yourself, you'll see what an unbalanced relationship you really had.

29. It is natural to mourn a dead relationship. Try and restrict the length of the grieving period, by throwing yourself a pity party to get it all out of your system in one go. Pack up all your ex's belongings and courier it back to them.

30. Don't apologise for their shitty behaviour and take all the blame for the demise of the relationship. It takes two to tango, two to make a good relationship but only one to end a bad relationship. Write down the things you might have done wrong, the part you might have played and focus on changing them in your next relationship.

My late grandmother used to tell me, life is like a tapestry. You can only see the whole picture when the tapestry is complete. The dark threads represent the trials and bad times in our lives. The brightly-coloured threads represent the good in our lives. The dark threads make the brightly-coloured threads stand out more, so the bad helps to highlight the good, and make us appreciate it so much more. Isn't it better to have a rich life tapestry with lots of contrasting colours, than a bland dull one?

**Agateophobia- Fear of insanity.**

# CHAPTER 2
# Don't tell me this is happening to me again!

*You have nobody to blame but yourself if you stumble more than once over the same stump.*
    <u>Italian Proverb</u>.

The bar was crowded, but Rick made me feel like I was the only person there.  I looked at the bar counter where he was getting us another round of drinks – he had to be the most divine man in the room.  His muscles bulged in his tight-fitting black tee, everything about him was wonderful.  I still couldn't believe he was here with me, and kept pinching myself to make sure that I wasn't dreaming.

Rick was everything Jason was not.  We had the same sense of humour, same taste in food, music and sport, we were like clones of each other, except that he was hot and I was not.  When I was sick, he popped around unexpectedly with flowers and medication for me.  He fixed my broken vacuum cleaner, cleaned a pot I'd burnt.  Rick was definitely every woman's dream.  Jason had never done anything like that.  It all had to be about him, and don't even think of ever asking him to fix anything.  I'd always eventually have to do that myself.  My kids adored Rick, whereas they'd always been terrified of Jason and his temper tantrums.

Right from the beginning Rick was upfront about his status.  He told me he was semi-attached, in that he was still married, but they only stayed together for the sake of his son and they had been sleeping in separate rooms for the last 4 years. I still remember saying that I thought only houses could be semi-attached. After 3 months of seeing Rick, he started making excuses as to why we couldn't meet, I started catching him out in lies, and once he forgot to remove his wedding ring before he met me. By that stage, I was so smitten with him I could forgive and forget anything. Then his marriage broke up and he was devastated, and I used to chat to him for hours on the phone, trying to rebuild his self-esteem. He got custody of his son, and that became a convenient excuse as to why we couldn't go out at night, but we were best friends and still hung out a lot together.

Eventually I was cooking them meals to keep frozen in his freezer, taking his son with my family whenever we went anywhere, paying for everything, using my family's housekeeping money to buy them groceries and luxuries they couldn't afford. I spent thousands of dollars I could ill afford on Rick and his son. When I found out that Rick was seeing someone 10 years younger than me, I was devastated. I wanted to end our friendship completely, but he begged us to continue to be friends as I was his only best friend. So continued the next 3 years, with Rick giving just enough to keep me hanging on in hope. He took up so much of my time, there was no time left for other relationships, and I bought him a surround sound system, computer, laptop, stove, video camera and finally a 4x4.

When I was told that I had breast cancer, I decided to clean my life up completely and get rid of all the other cancers in my life – Rick being one of them. In an indirect way, he always made me feel not good enough, and the damage he did to my persona, was the same that Jason had done, but in a nicer way. The day before my surgery, I dumped Rick in the most dramatic fashion possible and took back the 4x4 I had given him. He was devastated and couldn't understand what he had done wrong.

He had stolen 3 years of my life, is what he had done, the same as Jason who had stolen 10 years of my life. Rick still phones me every once in a while, but I see now that he only used me, fed off my strength and energy until I was absolutely drained. I was always there for him whenever he needed me, but when I really needed him, he couldn't afford the time.

I thought we had started off equal, but we hadn't really, as it had also all started from his lies. He fed me the stories about his cruel mean wife, and I felt sorry for him and did whatever I could to try to help him and make his life better. Rescuer and Victim game again. Once again I shifted from Rescuer to Persecutor to Victim. Same game, just different players. This has happened to me twice now, never again I vowed.

3 Months later I bought a house on a mortgagee sale, and inherited the owner/builder with it. Not in a relationship relationship, but more in a business relationship. He had a girlfriend who used to hassle

him a lot, text messaging him literally every 5 minutes. She wanted to know where he was every minute of the day. Dave enjoyed hanging round the house he'd built and promised to help complete it as it was only 75 % complete. Dave used to enjoy my company and would hang around quite a bit, telling me about his cruel mean ex-wife, and his controlling girlfriend. I felt sorry for him. He'd lost everything, and I thought maybe I could help him get back on his feet again. I lent him Rick's 4x4 I had taken off him, gave him a cellphone and let him do jobs for my company. He got everybody's back up, my other tradesmen, children and even customers, but I continually made excuses for him, saying he'd been through such a rough time, give him a chance.

It wasn't long before I discovered he also told very big lies, and he had a temper like Jason's. But I thought as I wasn't really in a relationship with him, it was okay to help him get back on his feet. However, he drained all my energy which was still recharging from the whole Rick debacle. Eventually, after he threatened to put my eldest daughter in hospital and tried to break the door down when my children wouldn't let him in when I was out, I terminated all dealings with him. Dave wouldn't return my 4x4 and broke into the house and stole a lot of my stuff.

Don't be fooled by a charming smile.

Because the house had once belonged to him, he viewed all the contents as his possessions. When I eventually got the 4x4 back, to say I was shocked was putting it mildly. Rick had kept it in mint condition, and it was in mint condition - hardly been used at all - when I'd lent it to Dave. The vehicle I got back was completely trashed. One whole side had been smashed in. The front showed evidence of bumping into something, his children had used a sharp instrument to scratch noughts and crosses games all over the car's body, there were other scratches all over the body where he'd obviously driven the vehicle in places vehicles shouldn't be driven, the CD player/stereo and speakers had been removed, the interior had stars scratched into it and the back chairs were broken. Luckily I was insured, and the insurance had no alternative but to write off the vehicle.

Once again, I had started off as the Rescuer, helping the poor Victim, and had ended up as a Victim myself.

I couldn't believe that something like this had happened to me yet again, and it didn't take much thought to see that there was a pattern here. I seemed to be getting involved with the same kind of people, relationship-wise and business-wise. People who started out as one thing, but in a month or so started to show that what they first portrayed, wasn't really their true self. I began to wonder, does everybody lie just to get in? Does this kind of thing happen only to me? Am I the only gullible fool in the universe, because when these things happen to me, all the people close to me say, "I told you so. We could see them for what they were and tried to warn you."

George Santayana (1863-1952), a US philosopher and poet, once said, "Those who cannot remember the past are condemned to repeat it." That's a truism if there ever was one. If we never take time out to try and understand our relationship history, and try and gain some understanding why we keep going for the same kind of person and ending up in the same kind of relationships, then we just remain in the loop letting history keep repeating itself, until we see the pattern and make the change. Nobody can change us, only we can. My life philosophy has always been, that life is just a series of adventures. Some adventures are good and some are bad. You take out what you can from each adventure and reflect - , what can I learn from this adventure to prepare myself for another adventure further down the track. Now, I have to ask myself, why am I having to repeat certain adventures? It seems as if I am stuck in a loop or something. Because I am obviously not learning from a bad adventure and not taking anything with me to prepare myself for a similar one down the track. I make the same mistakes every time and act true to form.

My eldest daughter said, that she believes that life is like a school. We keep getting given the same lessons over and over again, until we learn it, master it, and pass it and then only do we move onto the next lesson.

When I started talking to people about this pattern, of attracting the wrong kind of people, it turned out that I am not alone and many other people seem to do the same thing. How many people do you know, who leave one abusive relationship, only to go straight into another abusive relationship? Sometimes the abuser might seem so different to the previous one at the start, that even you are fooled for a time, but sooner or later they slip right back to type. And, haven't you noticed that it is always the genuinely nice people who care about other people, who are always the ones who get hurt. Does this tell us to stop caring about other people? Or does it make you ask the question, why are they sacrificing their own needs for other people? What are they really trying to avoid?

I have a friend who got involved with a woman 20 years older than himself at his work. He moved in with her and they've been together for over 20 years. He saw that she suffered from depression, so he thought he could help her. It didn't take him long to discover she was an alcoholic, and when drunk, she would verbally and emotionally abuse him. He's still with her today, as he doesn't want to leave their dogs behind, so he says.  But this same man, has had other flings on the side.  The one lady seemed to be everything he dreamed of, successful, intelligent, funny and very beautiful.  He couldn't believe his luck that she wanted him, so, he set her up in an apartment.  She resigned from her job and for the last few years he has paid her rent and living costs every month.  They no longer have a relationship, but he still pays for her.  When he found out that this lady was just using him, he met someone else, and set her up in an apartment as well, paying all her living expenses and giving her pocket money.  They no longer have a relationship, but he feels an obligation to keep paying her way as he feels she wouldn't be able to survive without his help.

This poor man is now paying for 3 needy women to live the good life, while he works all hours to earn the money to keep them, and he isn't really having a relationship with any of them.  They also keep him so busy with their needs and wants, that he doesn't have the time, or the money to get involved with anybody else.  This is a man of genius – well above average intelligence.  You ask yourself, why doesn't he just dump them and move on.  The answer is because he feels a responsibility towards them, and I believe that in some strange way it feeds his ego and gives him a feeling of power, but at the same time it is breaking him completely.   He is full of fear; fear of being alone, fear of not being needed. While supporting these three needy women builds up his self-esteem, it brings forward other fears - like how he is going to continue to meet his responsibilities in a world becoming more expensive by the day. He is definitely not a winner in this game!

My friend is also playing the Rescuer and Victim game, and as you can see, he has become a Victim. But he isn't just playing one Rescuer and Victim game, he is playing 3 games simultaneously! Should he end all dealings with those ladies, they wouldn't just curl up and die as he assumes they would without his help. They'd just find another Rescuer to feed off. The tragedy, is that all 3 of these ladies like to take on the role of Persecutor, and really let him have it from time to time, blaming him for everything that's gone wrong in their lives. Can you imagine the stress he must be under when all 3 play the Persecutor role at the same time! Poor bastard will move from one to the other, hoping to get peace and quiet, and just end up getting it in the neck.

You have to remember, that nice people can have backbones too. Sometimes being nice can make you a target. We always worry about whether or not we've done something to hurt the other person, but do we ever stop to think and consider, do they give a damn if they hurt us? You need to be nice to yourself, and take care of yourself first.

Jade was in an abusive relationship. Her partner was very possessive and didn't like her to have friends. He would refer to them as sluts and be rude to them if they visited. As time went by, family and friends popped around to visit less and less. The first time he got really angry, he would pin her against the wall. Eventually, he was punching her in the stomach whenever she 'disobeyed' him. If that wasn't bad enough, he started convincing himself that Jade was cheating, and would make up huge stories in his mind that sounded plausible. Whenever he accused Jade of infidelity, part of her started wondering if she was doing something wrong. One Sunday, he threatened her with a knife and forced her to admit that she'd been talking about him to her friends at work. Instead of letting her go, he kidnapped her, and drove around the streets saying he was looking for a suitable place to kill her. When he finally calmed down and took her back to their home, she took the day off work and packed up her stuff and left him and moved back in with her mother.

He threatened to do something bad to her mother if she didn't go back to him. Jade, not wanting to hurt her elderly mother, caved in and returned to her partner. The abuse continued. So did Jade's pattern of leaving him, only to return when he vowed to physically hurt her mother or friends. After the 2nd kidnapping incident, Jade filed a restraining order against him. He went for counselling, and started telling her how much he'd changed. Jade believed him, as she really missed him and loved him so much. This time, after being back a couple of months, Jade found out she was pregnant. The physical abuse stopped, but was replaced by verbal abuse. The least little thing she did would bring up past issues. It was as if he carried around a kitbag, and stored every little thing she'd done wrong in it. The minute she stepped out of line, the kitbag would be opened, and like Pandora's Box, all the bad things, hurts, insults, history would come flying out, thus putting Jade "back in her place". Jade managed to get a decent job, with a good wage, and started supporting the household more and more. She worked hard to rescue her little family, and her partner did less and less, and then took to blaming his failure to provide for the family on her. You can easily see the Rescuer Persecutor Victim roles being played out here. You might ask, if Jade was so unhappy, why did she keep going back? Why did she keep repeating the same bad adventure with this man? The answer is fear. Fear of being without a man, fear of what he might do to her, fear of what might happen to her family and friends, fear of loneliness...the list goes on.

Jessica always ended up being hurt in relationships. Without fail, she would meet a man wounded and heartbroken after a painful divorce. She'd let him move in with her, look after him, take care of him and work really hard at rebuilding his damaged self-esteem. Rather like I did with Rick. As soon as his self-confidence returned, he'd start an affair with another woman. He'd leave Jessica and she'd be all alone again. That is, until the next emotionally damaged man came along.

Why didn't she learn her lesson? Why did she keep following this pattern? Well, although she always ended up getting hurt and that is quite an unpleasant thing to keep happening to her, she did get some positives out of it as well. Often when you look back on things that happened to you in life, you often only remember the positives.  The positives Jessica got, were:

•   The instant intimacy you get when you develop a close bond with the other person when you take care of them.

•   The familiar comfort of being the Giver without any of the discomfort you get when you are trying to be a Receiver.

•   A sense of safety at the beginning of the relationship, when she was in control of it and calling the shots.

•   Most importantly, when helping these men, she feels important, useful, valued and loved.

Jessica mistakenly believed, that after her man recovers, he'll be able to look after her.  However, all he wanted, was to enjoy the free gift she gave him.  They both had different agendas and that's why these kinds of relationships always end up in disaster - with Jessica frustrated, disappointed and heartbroken; and the man all happy and healed, ready to embark on a 'real' relationship with someone else.  Jessica felt anger, sadness and fear as she was abandoned once again.  Her fairy tale ending collapsed as her Prince rode off into the sunset with someone else on the white charger with him. Her self-esteem has taken another hammering.  Jessica'll blame herself for not being good enough, rather than realise that she was following the wrong map.

It's easy to get lost in life and start following the wrong map.  It's because needy people are so easy to connect with.  If you take care of them, or shower them with attention - they'll follow you home.

Eleanor Roosevelt once said, "Nobody can make you feel bad about yourself without your permission." In a normal world, that's probably true.  Unfortunately, the Persecutors are geniuses at control, and can make us doubt our very being.  We need to stop giving people permission to make us feel bad about ourselves!

If you are intent on playing games, be aware of the following:
• Don't let yourself be the Victim unless you have an underlying motive and are trying to achieve something specific.
• Be warned that if you play Rescuer you are often going to get hurt for your troubles.
• You can deliberately be a Rescuer with the intention of creating obligation in the Victim, or showing your power to the Persecutor.
• This game can often turn into a war-like situation, with friends and family taking sides.  Be aware that wars can often be very difficult to stop.
• A Rescuer is actually a Victim in disguise.


The big question, is if we know we play this game, then why do we continue playing it?  Well, most of us don't really realise that we play this game.  We just believe that we have the most abominable luck when it comes to relationships, and we send out the wrong signals and pheromones to attract the wrong kinds of people. It can't possibly be us who are at fault and have the problem, I mean, we are the good guys, aren't we? Which takes us to the Poor Me Syndrome.

**Alektorophobia- Fear of chickens**

# CHAPTER 3
## Oh woe is me and other pity parties

The two women were so engrossed in their conversation, that they didn't realise that their lattes were getting cold. The one woman appeared to be listening intently, while the other spoke non-stop in an excited manner, barely stopping every now and then to catch a breath. The listener punctuated the other's tirade with an "Oooo", or "Really?" or "I can't believe it!" every once in a while.

At another table in Starbucks, a couple were sitting just as engrossed in their conversation. The man was gesticulating with his hands as if trying to prove a point, and the women was listening with a sympathetic expression on her face. It was a Monday morning, and the coffee shop seemed to be full of people sharing their news about their weekend. I looked around and took in the whole scene as I waited for my friend to arrive. It seemed to me, that a lot of the news being told were dramas, judging by the expressions on the listener's faces. I suddenly realised that I was attending an open invitation pity party, and felt a little guilty that I was about to dump all my weekend dramas on my friend as soon as she arrived.

But, "Whatever," I thought to myself. The weekend's dramas were far too juicy not to share, and my friend expected to hear all the latest developments anyway. Margie often told me that my life was better than Shortland Street, and she seemed to enjoy hearing all about the bad luck that seemed to follow me. Eventually she arrived, hung her jacket over the back of her chair, and placed her elbows on the table, looking at me expectantly. Far be it for me to disappoint her, so I opened my mouth and it all rushed out.

The Pity Party and Poor Me Syndromes are all essential parts of the Rescuer and Victim game. When your energy is all sapped out, and everything becomes too much for you, you throw a Pity Party. Initially, you are the only person invited to this party, as you feel so sorry for yourself, you don't think of inviting anyone else. You believe you are so worthless, nobody would want to come and join in the 'fun'.

Part of being a Rescuer, is that you spend so much time helping the Victim with their problems, and solving their crises, that you don't pay any attention to your problems and they just mount up, silently, unbeknownst to you, in the background. Sooner or later, the bin holding these problems of yours overflows, and you look to the Victim you were helping, to assist you with your problems. After all, you deserve some help for all the help you gave, right? However, in typical Victim fashion, they abscond, leaving you like rats leave a sinking ship and move onto the next Rescuer. Sometimes, that Victim might even change roles and become the Persecutor, to persecute you and make your life even more miserable. Even worse, is when the Victim's Persecutor that you were trying to rescue them from, turns round and comes after you. The worst is, when you put so much effort into helping someone get back on their feet, and they turn on you and accuse you of ruining their life and taking away their independence.

Wow, isn't life so complicated when we play this game. Who said all games should be fun?

I can remember times when a big truck in front of my car looked so inviting, I had to consciously talk myself out of driving straight into it. There were other times when I wished I could turn into a bear and go into hibernation. I could wake up when everything was happy and good again. However, that is not reality or a way to solve problems. All you do is create more problems for those you leave behind. The good news, is that Rescuers don't slip into Pity Party mode for very long. We feel so sorry for ourselves, mope around as if we have the world on our shoulders, look so down and depressed. People constantly ask us what's wrong, and we always reply, "Nothing."

Part of being in the Pity Party mode, is being a martyr. Everybody can see that something is wrong, but you are brave and strong and can carry the world on your shoulders. I'm surprised that people don't have to spray air freshener when we walk into the room, as the smell of a burning martyr must be bad!

Rescuers are rescuers because they are strong and courageous, and that's what attracts the victims to them in the first place. Therefore, it is understandable, that they won't be victims for long and will soon move out of the Pity Party phase, into their next phase after playing Victim and Martyr. Rescuers are usually people who have good problem solving skills. I know, when faced with a problem, I soon think of a Plan A, B or C. Which is why -Jason, Rick and Dave and many others, offloaded all their problems onto me, so that I could think of solutions to solve it for them. The bonus of course, is that when I solved their problems, I could just file all my problems away in a 'To do later box'. But is that really a good idea? Experience has proved that it's not. Everybody elses' problems are sorted, and mine accumulate and get worse.

Go into any coffee shop and watch the people and see how many you can identify in the Poor Me Syndrome phase. The Poor Me Syndrome follows the Pity Party. The Poor Me Syndrome is where you simply just have to tell everybody about what you did to help somebody, how it all turned against you, and how you're suffering as a result. The listener will look at you with an incredulous expression, tell you how marvellous and fantastic you are for trying to help someone who didn't deserve to be helped in the first place, and sympathise with you now for the predicament you're in.

Poor Me Syndrome isn't about getting people to feel sorry for you, that's just one of the side-effects of the Syndrome. Poor Me Syndrome is all about getting people to recognise you for what you tried to do, people to admire you, respect you. You usually tell your listener to keep it in confidence, and blah…blah…blah…you blurt out everything. They empathise, tell you how wonderful you are, and subconsciously, you know that it's human nature to spread the news. The listener will tell everybody what sacrificial things you did to help someone, and everybody will be so supportive towards you for what you're going through now. This is the reward you look for when you go into Poor Me Syndrome – universal acknowledgement. "Look at me, poor me, look what I'm going through as a result…"

When you pick yourself up, recharge your batteries and move on and become strong again, everybody will admire you even more. People think that Poor Me Syndrome is all about you wanting people to feel sorry for you. They are so wrong, Poor Me Syndrome is wanting people to recognise you for your true worth. You want admiration and all this is, is an ego building thing. It has nothing to do with pity That is reserved for the Pity Party phase. Even then, it's not really pity you are after. You just want to be seen and recognised as someone special. In a nutshell, you build up your self-esteem on the backs of the Victims.

Listeners fall into the trap of getting caught up in the whole drama, and they think it's their role to offer the Poor Me Syndrome people advice on how to cope with the drama, what do to about the situation, and how best to rid themselves of the initial Victim. They are being dragged into the drama triangle as a rescuer!

You will be the only guest at your Pity Party.

What they don't realise, is that people with Poor Me
Syndrome aren't after their advice.  They are not
interested in it and nine times out of ten aren't going
to even use it.  People with Poor Me Syndrome are
just feeding off the Listener's energy and sapping
them dry, using their energy to recharge their batteries
and regain their strength.  Luckily, Poor Me Syndrome
is just a short phase of the Rescuer and Victim game
we play.

Unfortunately, on the down side,  many good
friendships end during this phase, when the listeners
get tired and frustrated of listening to problems, giving
advice that isn't taken, and hearing the same stories
over and over again.  It can be tedious for them and is
definitely exhausting and energy sapping.  No matter
how wonderful a friend you are in reality, the Poor Me
Syndrome can kill a good friendship.

How to throw yourself a pity party
Okay, so you're all upset and need to throw yourself
a pity party just to get the sadness and sense of defeat
out of your system.  That's all right as long as you
know when to stop the pity party, send the sad 'you'
away and then move on and get on with your life.  The
important thing is that your pity party is controlled and
doesn't get out of hand.  It is normal to feel sad and
sorry for yourself when things get too much or go
wrong.  It is good to let go of those emotions, rather
than holding onto them and bottling them up inside.
So, here's how to arrange a pity party for yourself.

DO NOT TRY THIS IF YOU ARE CLINICALLY DEPRESSED OR ARE ON MEDICATION FOR DEPRESSION.

1. Let a close friend know that you are planning a pity party' Invite them over to just be a presence in your home, but not sit with you while you have your party. Alternatively, arrange a time that they'll come round or phone you to help you end the party.

2. Remove any medications or potential weapons from your room.

3. Close the curtains and put on some mournful music.

4. Focus on all the things in your life that make you unhappy.

5. Think of all the little things that bother you.

6. Suspect everybody and think of what ulterior motives they might have.

7. Condemn yourself and others for not being perfect.

8. Get yourself a good worry and focus on it.

9. Compare yourself unfavourably to others.

10. Take everything people have said to you personally.

11. Blame yourself for everything that went wrong.

12. Have a good cry about everything. Make sure you have a box of tissues handy.

13. Get everything out of your system. Make sure you concentrate on everything that's made you unhappy in the past, so that unhappiness appears to be the aim of your life.

14. Now, change your focus and start thinking about what brings you joy, hope and happiness. What makes you laugh out loud? Think about plans you can make

to change whatever caused the pity party in the first place. Brainstorm all the pros and cons of all the options that you think would change the situation you are in. Have a pen handy and write them down.

15. Think about good things that have happened to you, however minor.

16. Open the curtains and let in some natural light.

17. Turn off the mournful music and put on some loud, energetic, dance music. Ppreferably one you know the words of and can sing along to.

18. Have a lingering bath or a shower and imagine that you are washing all the unhappiness and misery away.

19. Contact your friend you spoke to at the start of your pity party. Let them know that you're okay and arrange to share a coffee, slab of chocolate or wine or two with them.

20. Steer the conversation to happy topics and keep a smile on your face, however idiotic you might think it looks!

Pity parties are a good way to get rid of all your bad feelings. People who tend to bottle everything up inside themselves, do tend to explode at a later date, usually at an inappropriate time. If you think of yourself as a kitbag, then all your past hurts, bad feelings and sad thoughts are all the 'junk' you stuff into the kitbag. Sooner or later that kitbag will be so full, that no more hurts can be stuffed inside it. It really is a good idea to empty it out occasionally. The trick, though, is not to stay in the pity party mode for too long. You don't want to end up with everbody avoiding you as they think you are a 'whining poor me' type of person!  Because, let's be honest here, people tend to gravitate towards happy positive people.  They'll be patient and listen to your whining up to a certain point, then they'll put you in the 'too hard basket'.

Needy People

Most people enjoy the thought of being needed at some point.  It makes them feel good and builds up their self-esteem.  But, there is a fine balance here between being overly needy and not being needy at all.  Some men view a lack of neediness in a woman as a fatal flaw and often accuse them of wanting to be men.  People who are overly needy, enjoy playing the Victim and just loll around waiting to be rescued.  After a while though, this excessive neediness can get wearisome for everybody else.

Abusive, controlling people rely on their partner to need them.  It gives them the power they crave.  So if you play the Needy Victim Game, you could be leaving yourself open to a whole lot of abuse.  The inability to have clearly defined needs, too many needs or no needs at all, are often symptoms of a co-dependent relationship.

I suppose it's a Men are from Mars and Women from Venus thing.  Men find 'being needed' a primary source of emotional security.  Their need is to feel important in their partner's life, and having a needy partner fulfills that need.  Women, however, tend towards 'being wanted' as their primary source.

Everybody at some time or other, when in a relationship, wants to be needed as a partner. It's like you're saying – "I can't do without you' which I suppose equates in the partner's mind to – "I desire you". I think the problem comes about in relationships where one partner is very 'in your face' independent, and goes out of their way to prove that they don't need anybody and are completely self-sufficient. It's like they throw off a vibe that says, "I was fine and self-sufficient when I met you and I'll be fine and self-sufficient if you go." This doesn't make for warm, fuzzy feelings in the other partner at all, because we have been conditioned to believe that if a person doesn't need you, then they don't want you.

So, if you have problems being needy as you're very independent, then pretend. Pretend you need help and advice from your partner. This will make them feel good, wanted and loved. If you are honest with yourself, you'll admit that you do need them in some sense, otherwise you wouldn't miss them if they go.

Don't try to be a superhero and do everything yourself. Share the load, start relying on your partner in some instances and enjoy a shared ride through life. The alternative, is a very lonely road.

Let me state, that I don't see not needing someone as a reason to go out and get therapy. There was a time when I needed a man to help me with the house renovations, mow the lawn, etc. But, if you don't have one, you have to survive, so you learn how to do things yourself.  If you don't do them, no fairy godmother or godfather is going to arrive and do them for you.  However, if you find yourself in a new relationship, you have to learn to share the load with your new partner and not make them feel left out and unwanted.  The key to a good relationship is balance.  Unbalanced relationships often drown in unhappiness and resentment.

**Angrophobia - Fear of anger or of becoming angry.**

# CHAPTER 4
## Superhero Syndrome.

As I stand on the top of the tall building, the wind catches my hair. My voluminous gold cape blows behind me in the cold air. To complete the picture I have on a tight-fitting muscle-hugging tee, tights, and over that - golden underwear. I watch and wait to do what is right. To help a poor soul and save them from their plight. I act in the day and sometimes at night, for I am......can we get a drum roll here? For I am.......**THE SUPER HERO of your life!** Yeah, that does sound rather good, doesn't it?

It's amazing though, we don't look on ourselves as super heroes, or see ourselves as suffering from Superhero Syndrome. That's the perception that other people have of us. "Look at Katy," they'd say, "She's so strong and courageous, I could never do what she does." We hear those comments of course, and feed off that, and that's what gives us the strength to continue.

You don't consciously set out to be a Superhero. It's not like you wake up one morning, and think, "Hey, think I might save the world today!" Basically, you are just a warm, caring generous kind of person who is prepared to go the extra mile to help others, and who is prepared to leave their own comfort zone from time to time in this quest. Many people do that, it's called compassion, and that doesn't necessary make them Superheroes or suffer

51

from Superhero Syndrome. What turns them into Superheroes, is when they do it time and time again, putting themselves and their families in danger and at risk, as the people they are helping are out of the norm. I am not talking about helping an elderly neighbour to carry in groceries here, or Superman flying through the air to thwart a bag-snatcher.

People who suffer from Superhero Syndrome have an addiction, like smoking, or drugs or alcohol, or sex. Oops, did I say that? They are addicted to helping people and it becomes a fix they need in life. They need to be constantly helping others to make themselves feel whole and alive. Helping others makes them feel worthy of being on this planet in the first place. Helping others gives them a purpose in life. It gives them a feeling of control, and it gives them an excuse to shelve their own problems. "No time for my problems, I'm on a mission to save someone else!"

Being a Superhero is just another form of escape from yourself. You have no time to deal with 'you' or your issues, you are too busy taking on everybody elses. The more you prove to everybody that you can solve their problems, the more problems they'll present for you to solve. Rescuers constantly go places, do things, participate in activities they don't

Superhero Syndrome

really want to do, rather than upset people. You tend to compromise your own needs on behalf of others.

I can remember Rick being in tears over his problems with the IRD. They were after him for over $10 000 as he hadn't submitted a tax return or GST return for 3 years. He was being threatened with jail and was beside himself with fear. Rick was broke and didn't have money to go to an accountant or bookkeeper. "It wasn't my fault," he kept saying over and over again, "Rachel used to do my books, but when my marriage started going sour, she stopped doing them and I didn't know how to do them, so I left them." Well, let me tell you a little secret, I didn't have a clue how to do them either. But I didn't tell Rick that. So, I did what any Superhero would do, I offered to do them for him.

53

Rick was so relieved, and I asked him to bring all his books and paperwork around so I could do it for him. That was in the November. I hate nagging, so just dropped a subtle hint every now and then, that it might be a good idea for him to bring all the paperwork around. "No worries," he'd say, "No rush, as I told IRD you were doing it and I got an extension until March when the court case is." Well, 6 days before the court case, Rick brought all his paperwork around in 3 supermarket packets. None of it was filed in date order, let alone in year order. On top of looking after my family and working a 9 to 5 job, I spent just over 80 hours of my time in those 6 days, on completing 3 years books, tax returns and GST Returns. I was exhausted afterwards, but felt really good about myself. I had managed to sort out all his tax problems, get the $10 000 written off and also get him a refund! Needless to say, I did not even get a token packet of lollies or a slab of chocolate as a thank you.

The more I helped Rick, the more he needed my help. Every letter or phone call he didn't know how to deal with, I dealt with it for him. When his friends had IRD problems or needed letters written, he'd bring it round and I'd do it for them. His friends thought that he was wonderful, as he could get so much done! However, it all just plumb tired me out. Something had to give, and it was the time I spent doing my own paperwork that suffered and the time I spent with my children.

Looking back on my time with Jason, it was no different. He had an aversion to work, period. I cooked, cleaned, earned the money to keep us going and feed the family. I would do all kinds of crafts or extra things to make more money so we could have a few luxuries. Jason would just watch TV all the time or play games on the computer. He never worried about how to put food onto the table, as he knew that Katy would always make a plan. I remember being upset when at the end of my relationship with him, my mother-in-law told me that his laziness and failure to provide for the family was all my fault. She told me that I was an enabler, I enabled him to become like that as he knew that I would fly in as the Superhero to make everything right. He could be lazy and do what he wanted, I'd always provide. As cruel as it had seemed at the time, his mother was right. I'd enabled him to become lazy.

Initially, sufferers of Superhero Syndrome are expert jugglers. Time jugglers, that is. They are always busy, rushing here, rushing there, rushing everywhere. At first you can fit in and accommodate yours and your family's needs, but sooner or later, they take a back seat as your life revolves around the poor Victim you are helping. A Superhero is a very busy person. "No rest for the wicked," is a favourite saying I used while flying in and out.

However, all the 'busyness' wears you down, exhausts you and puts you into a downward spiral. As you help your Victim less and less, they move on, and leave you behind, or turn into a Persecutor and start blaming you for their demise. "If you didn't do everything I wouldn't be so dependent, so it's all your fault that I don't know how to do things." "You never have time for me anymore, and I don't have anybody else to ask to help me, so if you don't find the time to do it, I'll get into deep trouble and it'll all be your fault." And as Jason used to say to me quite often, "What can I say, you're a better man than I am," when I solved problems for him and sorted things out.

You recharge your batteries, vow never to do something like that again, promise family and friends this is it - no more helping people like that, never ever ever again, and so on. I wonder why they just nod and smile and don't believe you? And, they are right. Because sooner or later, like a junkie, you need that fix. "I have to help someone, have to save someone, have to change someone's life for the better!" So, you dig your golden cape out of the bottom of the cupboard, iron out the wrinkles and creases and there you go! A for away!

Please don't misunderstand me, it's not wrong to help people, but it is wrong to do too much for people that you are actually harming them more than you are helping. The difference between helping and rescuing, is that in helping you are assisting that person. It is a joint effort and they are contributing

56

something towards it.  In rescuing, the other person is doing nothing and all you're actually doing – is helping them to continue doing nothing.  Remember, that pity generates pitiful persons.

It is also not a good idea to shelve your family and friends, and things that you need to do while you are out on a mission to help somebody else.  Sometimes, we don't want to spend time with ourselves, that's why we fall into Superhero Syndrome.  Being busy all the time means that you never have time to be alone with yourself.  What are you trying to hide from yourself or run away from?  What fears are driving you?  If you find yourself trapped in the Superhero cycle, you need to get out.  I found out the hard way, that doing things for people, doesn't guarantee their love and respect, and doesn't even necessary make them like you as a friend.  You are just setting yourself up to be used and abused.  That is a lose/lose situation, and there are no winners in that Game.

**Arachibutyrophobia- Fear of peanut butter sticking to the roof of the mouth.**

# CHAPTER 5

## Show them how to fish

*Give a man a fish and you feed him for a day. Teach him how to fish and you feed him for a lifetime.*

Chinese Proverb

*Build a man a fire, and he'll be warm for a day. Set a man on fire, and he'll be warm for the rest of his life.*

Terry Pratchett

Jessie threw back her head, stamped her foot, and put her lips into a fish pout. "Here we go again," I thought to myself, "I wonder when she'll ever grow out of the sulks?"

"Why do you ask me to do the dishes, when you know I don't do them properly," Jessie complained. "I try my best but I just can't do them, and then Matt teases me and Lisa has a tantrum and shouts at me because there's some left over food from last night still on her plate!" Jessie looked at me accusingly and I just sighed.

"Ok, get out of the kitchen, I'll do it," I say in desperation just to get it done. Jessie runs up to me, "Thank you Mummy, you're the best!" If I am the best then why don't I feel the best?

There is a very thin line between being a Superhero who does everything to help people, and being a martyr. Too often we jump from one to the other. What I should have said to Jessie was, "Come here, let

Mummy show you how to do the dishes properly. You can help me this time, and next time you'll be able to do it all by yourself!"

In retrospect, I should have told Rick, you sort all your receipts into years, months and date order, because let's get real here – any monkey could do that if they had to. It doesn't take any real brain power, just time and energy. If I could work out how to do a set of books, then he could too. I could have just sat down with him and helped him do the first couple of months, and then he could have done the other 34 months by himself!

As humans we are innately lazy creatures, if we can get someone else to do something for us without us having to use our time and energy, then we will. And, as innately lazy creatures, if we think it's quicker to just do something ourselves rather than show someone how to do it and risk having to redo it if they get it wrong, then that's what we'll do. Then they'll never learn and we'll just continue doing everything ourselves.

The trick here, is not to leave your Victim alone to drown, but to be there as support and show them how to save themselves. That way, if they land in the same situation again, they'll know what to do. Many people, (I won't say what sex at the risk of getting my head chopped off, and I'm not ready to die just yet), make a half-hearted attempt to do something themselves, but they set themselves up to fail, knowing that they are not going to do it properly. What happens? You clench your teeth, roll your eyes and do it properly yourself. What have they learnt? If

I make a half-hearted attempt to do it and fail, then I'll never be asked to do it again. This is what happens with our relationships with our children, our partners, and often our workmates.

I remember asking Jason to put up a shelf when I first moved in with him. Don't ask me why, but I just took it for granted that all men know how to use a hammer and put up a shelf. He hit his fingers a couple of times with the hammer, and had to take a few breaks to put ice on his thumb, and have a couple of beers. About 3 hours later - the shelf was up! It was slightly skew, but I told him how great it was, to try and build up his self-esteem – the loving caring person that I am. I picked up one of my daughter's fluffy toys that couldn't even have weighed a kilo, tops, and placed it gently on the shelf. As I turned around to pick up another toy to put on the shelf, the whole shelf came down with a crash! Jason threw his hands up in the air, "I'm such a failure! I fail at everything, everything I touch turns to shit!" It was quite a dramatic scene, this 6 foot 4 man on the verge of tears, because I'd forced him to put up a shelf that wasn't within his capabilities. Of course, as the Rescuer, I consoled him, told him he had many other talents, handyman stuff just wasn't one of them, and I slipped into the Superhero mode, and put up the shelf in 10 minutes. Guess what, it didn't fall down but stayed flush against the wall – and with my daughter's toys and books on it as well!

Jason's reaction to that was his usual sarcastic comment generated especially to hurt me, "Well, what can I say, you're a better man than me!" The truth is,

I'd never put up a shelf before in my life. I just worked it out logically, and Jason's sarcastic acknowledgement of what I'd done stung for a while. But what we learnt from that incident, very early on in our relationship, was that he couldn't do any maintenance or handyman work around the house as he was bad at it, and it was best if I did it all as I could work out how to do it. Once again it comes down to, make a half-hearted attempt to do something, make sure you fail, and you'll never be asked to do it again.

Unfortunately, in life, there isn't always a Rescuer or Superhero on hand to help you out and do things for you. You have to learn how to do them yourself. The best way to learn, is to have someone show you and teach you how to do it for yourself. Then in turn, you can show others how to do it and so on. That makes everybody more independent, evens out the workload, and enables people to have the time to spend with themselves and their family and friends.

Of course, there are people who thrive on the feelings of power they get when they control everything and have all these dependent people under them. They hold the mastery of how to do something close to their chests as they dread the day they lose that power. Those people generally have issues and low self-esteem, and hide behind their power, surrounding themselves with people they consider weaker than themselves, in an effort to make themselves appear stronger than what they are. They are just hiding their fears from the world. It's just another game they're playing. It's not the Rescuer and Victim game we play. 'Showing them how to fish' is a good way to leave the game, and the end result is win/win.

Laura was in a state. She had gone into panic mode. She had offered to organise a friend's farewell bbq. The day before the big bbq arrived and Laura had done nothing. 60 Guests were expected to attend. All were expecting a great party as they farewelled their friend on their big OE. Laura phoned Janice in tears, and asked her to please step in and arrange and organise everything for the bbq the next day. Through her tears, Laura told Janice what a wonderful organiser she was, and that every party she arranged was the best. She told Janice that she was useless at organising anything and never knew where to start. But, Janice on the other hand......

We can see that Laura is an ace at manipulation, and very very good at playing the helpless victim role. Most Rescuers/Super-heroes can't resist stepping in to help after their egos have been stroked like that. Because, now that we know what we know, if we were Janice, we wouldn't step in to help. Would we? WOULD WE? Sorry, just checking. So, if we weren't going to help, what would we do? We couldn't just leave Laura stranded like that? After all, she's a friend, and she'd tell everybody that the party was a flop because you refused to help.

If Janice had stepped in to help, Laura would just have taken a backseat and let her do everything. Janice would have gotten completely stressed out, then gone into martyr mode, and Laura would have learnt nothing. A potential lose/lose situation.

So, here's what Janice did. She asked Laura questions so that she could solve her own problems. Janice guided Laura a little when she got lost. She made Laura draw up a list of what needed to be done. Janice asked her what things were really urgent and got her to prioritise the list. Laura brainstormed what food was going to be served at the bbq. Janice got her to think of solutions as to how she was going to get all the salads etc made.

You'll notice, that Janice wasn't doing things for Laura. She was being supportive. Laura learnt how to solve the problems for herself. In 'showing her how to fish', Janice changed a lose/lose situation - into a win/win situation. Now, try and use these techniques with your partner, when you identify the times you both are playing The Game.

**Athazagoraphobia- Fear of being forgotten or ignored or forgetting.**

63

# CHAPTER 6
# THE CHECKLIST CHAPTER

All this talk of Victims, Persecutors and Rescuers, makes one think of the little deviations to The Game and the other games that get played on a daily basis. Although it's not a good idea to put people into boxes, and to be honest, most of us don't fit into any one box perfectly anyway, we are often a mixture of a couple of different boxes. That's what makes us unique. However, I've decided to incur the wrath of strangers and do it anyway.

**What we have to remember when we play games, is this:**

1. Although it may seem like it at the time, no-one actually wins.

2. These games cause pain and come from denied pain and fears.

3. They are about lies and unhealthy secrets.

4. They come from feelings of unworthiness and low self-esteem.

5. They are about a loss of personal power and identity.

6. They are derived from a perverted and distorted view of love.

7. The games are fed by people's guilt and fears.

8. They keep us caught in the loop of dysfunctional behaviour

9. Worst of all, our children watch us and learn our behaviours.

This chapter helps you to recognise which role you play in the Game of Life. Which one are you most like?

**Veronique the Victim**
· Has a low self-esteem and feelings of being unworthy
· Feels sorry for themselves
· Gives in at the first sign of a threat, avoids confrontation and is unable to stand up for self
· Believes their needs don't count
· Can't take responsibility for their own feelings or actions
· Can't make or stick to decisions
· Is often over-sensitive and very anxious
· Truly believes they can't take care of themselves
· Makes excuses for remaining a Victim
· Will actually lie to themselves about their ability to change their situation
· Will convince you they had 0% responsibilty for their Victimhood
· Can be very manipulative
· Uses 'Poor me' and 'Blame' to evoke sympathy which is another way of getting attention
· Feels that life hasn't been fair to them, but they are too scared to risk making the changes to move forward
· May have had an over-protective parent who led them to believe they were helpless, or an over-anxious parent who would lose the plot whenever their child had to suffer because of mistakes they made
· Gifted Victim will convince you their problems are yours

· A Master Victim will engineer his problems to become your problems

**Roger the Rescuer**
· Has a low self-esteem
· Builds up their self-esteem by being seen as unselfish for someone else's good
· Often has mixed motives
· Uses rescuing to connect with others or to feel important
· Uses rescuing to reduce their own feelings of anxiety
· Rescuing becomes an excuse not to address their own problems
· Feels guilty when not involved with other's problems
· Loses their self to meet others' needs and this causes depression
· Feels that the Victim owes them for all they've done for them
· Believes that because they have always willingly helped others, people will help them in return when they need it, but it rarely happens
· Sooner or later they start to feel that they are being taken advantage of, and then become a Martyr or Victim themselves
· Rescuing can become addictive as it makes them feel good at the expenses of others' rights to take care of themselves

**Colin the Control-freak**
· Tries to boost their low self-esteem by trying to control everything around them

· Believe that they have the task of protecting the world from mistakes

· Usually unaware that it's their fears that drives their behaviours

· Obsess about every tiny detail to try and keep a safe distance from mistakes

· Risk takers scare them

**Cameron the Commitment-Phobic**

· 'The grass is always greener on the other side' is their life motto.

· Will go all out to snare you and will be very attentive, then will start to come up with excuses as to why they cannot make a date

· They will avoid at all costs, any talk or discussion of any troubling issues in your relationship

· They will always tell you how 'busy' they are

· Will often have been badly hurt by someone in the past, so will subconsciously hide behind their wall every time someone gets too close for comfort

· Might have a fear of getting old, and getting seriously involved with someone, means settling down, and in their eyes settling down means losing their youth.

· Could have had a childhood growing up in an abusive family environment, or have been a pawn in a bitter divorce

· Most feel bad when they hurt others emotionally

**Paula the Persecutor**

· Gives the impression that they feel superior to others

· Gets high on the adrenalin rush when fighting and witnessing fights

· Anger and self-righteousness seems to give them the energy to ward off depression

· Needs to be in control and will use verbal abuse to keep in control

· Uses anger to cope with threats, new ideas and conflicts

· Releases stress by blaming, criticizing and attacking others

· Very judgmental of others and gets annoyed when they don't do what they say

· Believes that nothing will happen if it wasn't for them and they are 200% responsible for any good thing that happens

· Believes that everybody 'owes' them

· They deny their own weaknesses and use anger to cover them up

· They will always find reasons to make others wrong and will even go so far as to turning them into a scapegoat

· Believes that others deserve the abuse and punishment they dish out.

· Could either have had a parent who spoiled them and always gave them their own way, or who was aggressive and showed them how to win by using force

**Billy the Serial Bully**

· Pathological liar who can make up a convincing lie at the drop of a hat

· Has a split personality - nasty, spiteful and vengeful in private and to their current Victim, and charming and innocent in front of others

· Very good at using excessive charm to deceive others, so nobody believes the poor target of the serial bully when they try and report their actions

· Shallow, superficial and has the ability to verbally outmanoeuvre anybody

· Will always suck up to their superiors

· Has a good memory and is able to memorise material and feed it back in such a convincing way, that they can convince people they actually did it, used it or saw it

· Very good at anticipating what people want to hear

· Is all talk and usually can't be relied upon or trusted to fulfill their commitments

· Is emotionally immature and often displays emotional age of a five year old, but has the language and intellect of an intelligent adult

· Is incapable of initiating or sustaining intimacy in a relationship

· Often shows unusual and inappropriate attitudes towards sex and bodily functions, and this is used to discriminate against and harass others

· Self-opinionated and arrogant and makes prejudicial comments about other races, gender, religions, homosexuals in private, and are charming towards those people in public

· Is a control-freak and will poison people's minds to manipulate their thoughts and emotions.

· Very good at creating conflict and then moving aside to become the caring supportive observer

· Will target people who see through them and will turn their lives into a living hell

·     Are convinced that they are born leaders, but will resort to bullying tactics when placed in a leadership role

·     Always a taker and never a giver

**Ron the Rationaliser**

·     Cut off from their feelings and go inside their head to figure things out.

·     Protect themselves from feeling emotions at all costs.

·     Attract people who display the emotions they're holding on to.

·     People they attract will press their buttons to get them in touch with their buried emotions.

·     Will stop attracting button pressers once they've expressed their emotions.

Harry the Human Predator

**Harry the Human Predator**

·     Often have the appearance of having a healthy self-esteem and come across as confident, but it's often a facade to hide the frightened child inside

· Power hungry who wants everything their own way and doesn't mind underrating and humiliating others

· Choose to take advantage of others because they can and because it is often still within the limits of the law

· Has no conscience

· Destroys a person's virtues and then inflicts emotional pain on them

· Believe that they have a right to destroy and take advantage of those weaker than them, as that is the law of nature - only the strong survive

· Many are drug dealers, pimps, quacks, faith healers, and con artists who thrive on human greed

· Control, manipulation, domination and making lots of money are their goals

**Patrick the Player**

· Appears to have a high opinion of themselves, but this often hides a low self-esteem

· They continually have to prove themselves to others and themselves

· Is also commitment-phobic

· Seldom believes in monogamy

· Don't care if they hurt other's feelings

· They look on cheating on a spouse as a sign of intelligence and worthiness, and something to be proud of

· They are only interested in a person's outward appearance and have no interest in getting to know the real person inside

· Are incredibly shallow

**Emily the Enabler**

- Shields their partner from the harmful consequences of their behaviour
- Avoids conflict and will do whatever to keep the peace
- Will keep secrets about their partner's bad behaviour from others
- Will always make excuses for their partner's bad behaviour and blame others and try and evoke sympathy for them
- Constantly fixes up their partner's problems by bailing them out each time
- Claims to have a deep understanding of their partner, and will claim that the problem is a result of a bad childhood, shyness, abuse etc
- Avoids and hides away from the dependent partner when things get too much
- Gives out money that is undeserved and unearned
- Assumes the role of caregiver so dependent partner no longer has to do anything for themselves
- Makes threats that are never followed through
- Attempts to control the dependent partner by planning their lives for them

**Nora the Nazi**
- appears friendly
- lacks self-esteem
- has no friends
- hovers in the background unnoticed, picking up information
- feels it's their duty to report the information they picked up
- they feel good only when they get someone else into trouble

·     usually in the background somewhere gloating when the proverbial shit hits the fan

·     will pretend to be supportive, while looking for another knife for your back

·     often workaholics or compulsive and obsessive about something, as that is what they live for, having no social life

Nora the Nazi

## Chris the Co-dependent

·     Usually overly responsible and emotional

·     Is dependent on their partner emotionally, but the dependency is hurtful, emotionally stunted or keeps them from moving forward

·     Puts other's needs before their own, and has tendency to live their life through another or for another

·     Blames others for everything wrong in their life or with themselves

·     Tries to control others and circumstances around them by using force, threats, blackmail, advice giving, helplessness, laying down guilt trips, insulting, removing assets, selfishness, denial - anything to manipulate the other to maintain control

· Will accuse the other partner of being the controlling one

· Often has emotional problems like depression, anxiety, insomnia, addictions, obsessive behaviour in relationships

· Constantly seeks approval from their partner and has no sense of self-identity outside the relationship

· Scared and uncomfortable when alone

· Low self-esteem and very self-critical and has many fears

· Tends to be Rescuers and actively seek out those who 'need' them

· Have a poor set of boundaries and have problems setting limits for themselves and for others

· Attempts to 'fix' others or run their lives for them, often inappropriately

· Have a strong need to take care of others, but still have the false belief that the other person is responsible for them

**Destiny the Serial Dater**

· Is commitment-phobic and will find any excuse to dump their partner if they get too close

· Silly things might put them off a person, like the way they comb their hair, or the shoes they wear…

· Will often spend the whole date talking about themselves, how lonely they are and why they can't ever seem to find the right one for them

· Deep down they don't believe they are worthy and also believe they don't deserve to be fancied by someone, and will often subconsciously sabotage potential relationships

· They have a fear of being hurt or rejected, so have built a big wall around their heart

**Neville the Narcissist**

· Often comes from a family where they were ignored, so they crave attention

· Present a false self to the world which is one of arrogance and they are better than everybody else

· Has inner emptiness and many fears which they try and hide behind their false self, fears of being unwanted, unlovable, inferior and inadequate

· Has a tendency to exaggerate their accomplishments and boast about things to try and make people admire them

· Very dependent on other's approval, so are overly sensitive and will turn nasty if they think there is any hint of criticism, and will even go so far as to plan out a revenge attack

· Self-absorbed, shallow and emotionally immature so has problems having personal relationships

· Has created a fantasy world where they can entertain their dreams of greatness, although their dreams are usually unrealistic, however, they often convince themselves that they have attained their unrealistic dreams

· Will sometimes offer to help others, but this is usually for sake of appearance only

· Most people see through the Narcissist and hand them out their biggest fear - rejection

**Abe the Abuser**

· Has a low self-esteem

·    Have a fear of letting anyone get close to them as this makes them feel insecure

·    Has a compulsive need to always be in control and has the tendency to become control-freaks

·    Can be likeable and present themselves well, but they are broken inside and the person they present to the world is not the real person they are

·    They tend to have little or no clue that they have a problem

·    They can always come up with good reasons for their bad behaviour, and say that they were provoked and had no option but to behave in an angry way

·    They are always right and can justify their temper tantrums by blaming their partner

·    Their initial provocations are unseen by others, but their partner's reactions  are more visible and to friend's and family, the abused partner might seem at fault

·    They abuse their partner when things are going well to stop them from getting too close, as they believe if you let someone get too close, then you open yourself up for hurt

·    They expect their partner to be available to their every need 24 hours a day no matter what, and will 'punish' their partner if they are not available

·    Self-absorbed and often set high expectations which can't be met, so they take their disappointments out on their partner

·    Relationship is focused solely on meeting their emotional needs and they display no interest in meeting their partner's emotional needs

· Tend to take everything personally and to feel that people are blaming them, and will resort to extreme measures to prove that things are not their fault

· Often the victim of abuse themselves, or emotional neglect because of parent's addiction or illness, or difficult life so far

· Have never learned that it's okay to make mistakes or be imperfect

· Have learned to take things personally and to always feel others are blaming them, so they resort to extreme measures to prove that they are not at fault.

**Avril the Addict**

· Lacks willpower and will easily let a substance or person take control of their life

· Low self-esteem, has lots of anxieties and fears, and the addiction serves as a crutch to make them feel good, however temporarily

· Takes no steps to end the relationship even if they know it's bad for them

· Finds reasons to stay in the relationship which doesn't counteract the harmful effects it has on them

· Thoughts of ending the addictive relationship cause terrible anxiety and fear which makes them cling to it even more

· When they finally end the relationship, they might experience withdrawal symptoms which can even be physical pain, and this is only relieved by re-establishing contact

**Aunty Agatha the Advisor**

· has had, or knows of lots of experiences to draw from and is able to offer advice about most things

- usually means well, though can be seen as interfering
- might offer advice when not asked for it
- some enjoy saying, "I told you so"
- will give you options and possible solutions, but won't fix your problem for you.  That you have to do your self

**Geraldine the Gossipmonger**

- very social and has many friends
- favourite words are, "This is strictly in confidence"
- knows everything that is happening about everybody
- is a good source for information
- can be very gullible and will truly believe most things
- no mean intentions, just can't resist a juicy tale
- often their life is boring, so they get off on the dramas of others

**Richard the Rebel**

- Attention-seeking
- Has a low self-esteem and always has something to prove
- Deliberately has to be outrageous or do something outrageous to get attention
- They don't differentiate between positive or negative attention – in their eyes all attention is good
- Above all, all they really want is to be admired and loved
- Might have been the 'middle child' in the family, or had parents who were too busy to pay them the attention they deserved

**Larry the Layabout**

· Often have a low self-esteem and low sense of self-worth, believing that they are useless and can't do anything right

· Believe that it's better not to try, than risk trying and failing

· Are not risk-takers and seldom show initiative

· Will always have reasons for their bouts of laziness and it will never be their fault

· Are quite happy to watch others working, and seldom feel guilty about not pulling their weight

**Mick the Best Mate**

· Very popular and social being

· Prefers same sex company

· Would rather go out for a night on the town with mates, than stay home with their partner

· Will bring home their buddies without asking if it's okay first

· Mates' needs are far more important than their partner's

· Can get nasty when stopped from going out with mates

· Friends all believe that there must be something wrong with the 'stay-at-home' partner

**Pete the People Pleaser**

· Low self-esteem

· People take advantage of them

· Often feels unappreciated

· Has problems supervising others as doesn't like upsetting people or making people not like them

· Time management becomes an issue and they might reach burnout

- Lose their personal identity
- Don't know how to relax and have problems making decisions
- Struggle to accept kindness from others, prefer to do all the giving
- Often insecure with others and this has a negative effect on their interpersonal relationships
- Disorganised and come unglued under pressure
- Has a compulsive need to please others which is derived from their many fears
- Avoids conflicts and fights at any cost
- Denies that there are problems, everything is always all right, even when it isn't
- Insecure about their abilities and often run themselves down to friends
- Always smiling and interested in other's welfare
- Ready to take on any new challenge that comes along
- Ready to volunteer. Accepts delegation and is the ultimate team player
- Easy to get along with, helpful and supportive. Always ready to go along with requests made by others makes them popular, warm caring people

**Sarah the Scammer**
- Always on the look out for the main chance
- Often befriends those they feel are weaker than themselves, or who have something they want or can use
- Often has a good self-esteem and can come across as quite confident

· Will pretend to be suffering from 'Poor Me' Syndrome, to get people to feel sorry for them and then give them things

· Never worries about hurting other's feelings, or misplacing their trust

· Whatever they have is never enough, and they always want more, and will use and abuse whoever to get it

**Mandy the Manipulator**

· Crafty, cunning and is an ace at reading situations

· Great actor, and can play any role to get what they want

· Is the master of mind games

· Can be very subtle and very persuasive

· Uses blame a lot to make people feel guilty and do what they want

· Loves to play the 'Persecutor' role in the Drama Triangle

**Denise the Drama Queen**

· Low self-esteem

· Needs to be the centre of attention to feel good

· Moves from one drama to the next

· Has ability to turn any situation into a drama

· Usually a good storyteller and can keep a crowd entertained

· Can use this as a ploy to attract a Rescuer

· Might occasionally exaggerate the details to improve the drama

**Simon the Stubborn Mule**

· Has great persistence

· Never gives up even when adversities mount

· Often very proud

·    Not very good at asking for or accepting help

·    Not easily swayed from their beliefs, even if they are wrong

·    Low self-esteem so constantly trying to prove a point

·    Many admire their doggedness, but others find it frustrating

**Sam the Self-Destructor**

·    Very low self-esteem

·    Believes they are worthless and can't do anything right

·    Very poor self-image

·    Favourite saying is "Everything I touch turns to shit."

·    Very negative person

·    Believes they'll fail before they start something

·    Often will subconsciously sabotage something that might be succeeding

·    Lives permanently in pity party mode

·    Doesn't want help as they get off on sympathy

·    Others find them energy-sapping and tire of them easily

**Leo the Loner**

·    Can have a low self-esteem

·    Has often been badly hurt in the past and mistrusts other people and their intentions

·    Has built a humungous wall around their heart

·    Behind the wall is often a 'little child' just wanting to be loved, but is so filled with fear

·    Is a bit of a voyeur and would rather watch from a distance than take part

·    Believes there is safety in isolation

**Candice the Crusader**
- Low self-esteem
- Build themselves up by fighting for a cause
- Will take on another's problems to avoid dealing with their own
- Can let their cause become all-consuming, and neglect important matters concerning themselves
- Others admire them and this makes them feel good

**Marlene the Mindreader**
- Thinks that they always know what other people are thinking
- Will base their actions on their assumptions
- Always believes that they have assumed correctly
- Instinctively knows what's good for someone else
- Gets frustrated when people don't react the way they perceived
- Favourite words are, "But, I thought...."
- Might not give you information as they can foretell your reaction

**Ben the Bouncing Ball**
- Fears being tied down, but fears letting go
- Collects friends like others collect stamps
- Drops in out of the blue and resumes friendship
- Disappears again without a warning, leaving people wondering what they did to upset the bouncing ball
- Bounces in and out of relationships, never ending things, always leaving the door open to one day come back
- Often easily bored with same routine, so constantly looking for the thrill of a new beginning,

which they can keep having every time they bounce back into a relationship

· Need the security of having on/off relationships with people they know

**Pat the Procrastinator**

· Always puts off till tomorrow what needs to be done today

· Has problems prioritising things

· Files problems in the 'too hard basket' and plans on revisiting them later

· Easily distracted

· Very creative at finding excuses

· Will often keep putting off ending a relationship that's going nowhere

· Nothing is ever their fault

**Ian the Indecisive**

· Low self-esteem

· Has problems making choices and decisions

· Afraid of commitment to anything

· Relies on someone else to make the decision for them

· Believes that if they stick their head in the sand the problem will go away – Ostrich Syndrome

· Doesn't have fixed ideas or viewpoints, and can be easily swayed

· Scared of doing the wrong thing, so rather do nothing

· Might ask everybody's advice, and then still do nothing

**Hannah the Hope Stealer**

· Is a very negative person and will always point out the bad things in every situation

· Pretends to be well-meaning, while exaggerating the pitfalls you might face

· Is a very unhappy person with a low self-esteem, and will often go out of the way to infect others with their general unhappiness

· Will never let another enjoy their successes, but will always feel obliged to point out all the things which could go wrong or undermine that success

· Will always dash the hopes and dreams of another person

· Is filled with fear and too scared to take a risk or to have a dream themselves

**Dennis the Dreamer**

· Is an 'ideas' person

· Can imagine the end result, but often lacks the drive and determination to get there

· Has problems finishing what they start

· Can get depressed when things don't work out, but never stays down for long

· Can easily lose their focus if another dream gets in the way

· Can be very spontaneous

**Rick the Risk-taker**

· Is easily bored, needs constant challenges

· Is prepared to take a chance to improve their lot in life, and concedes that sometimes it might not work

· Able to think outside the square

· Very spontaneous

· Prepared to try everything at least once

· Might sometimes overlook potential pitfalls with dire results

**Desiree the Desperate**
·   Low self-esteem and poor self-image
·   Often attracted to the wrong kind of people
·   Will ignore abuse and cheating to hang on to their partner
·   'Having that particular person in their life' is their number one priority
·   Can become obsessive and smothering
·   Will do or endure whatever it takes to have that particular person
·   Will even go as far as re-inventing themselves for that person
·   Will never be truly happy as they aren't being true to themselves

**Peggy the Panic Pot**
·   Low self-esteem
·   Has many fears about a lot of different things
·   Has a negative outlook on life and always expects the worst
·   Suffers from anxiety and can get panic attacks
·   Gets easily stressed and loses focus
·   Only sees the problems and not possible solutions
·   Wants a Rescuer to fix things and take away the anxiety
·   Might wish hibernation was an option until the problem disappeared

**Julian the Judge**
·   Might have an overly good self-esteem
·   This gives them the right to criticise others
·   Nobody is as good as they are

·   They look down on others from their judge's bench, deciding who should be helped and who should be punished

·   People in their group might look up to them and follow their lead

·   They can have a lot of influence, into who is allowed in their group

·   Can be unforgiving, don't get on their wrong side

**Mary the Mediator**

·   Has a good self-esteem

·   Very level headed and well-balanced

·   Has good problem solving skills

·   Able to see both sides of a disagreement, and give impartial advice

·   Is emotionally mature

·   People confide in the Mediator

·   Is often called upon to act as a go-between

·   Has a sympathetic nature, but is not a Rescuer

**Ingrid the Internet Lover**

·   Very low self-esteem

·   Might be shy in face-to-face situations

·   Will have been hurt or suffered rejection in the past

·   Prefers meeting people on the internet, as gives them a

    feeling of control

·   Able to live out fantasies which they are too scared to try in real-life

·   Can hide behind the screen if they are self-conscious about their looks

·   Finds safety in associating with strangers

·    Often have no intention of meeting the people they chat to

·    Having an internet partner/friend, gives them a sense of belonging and having someone to care about

·    Can be very lonely and very unhappy with their life

·    Becomes anti-social, turning down invitations, to stay at home in front of the net

·    They are more confident with the safety of the screen between them the stranger on the other side

**Brenda the Busy Bee**

·    Low self-esteem

·    Permanently multi-tasking and always under pressure

Ingrid the Internet Lover

·    Appears to thrive on pressure, but the truth is - it's a back-up excuse in case something fails.  Too much to do so not their fault

·    'Busyness' stops them from spending time with themselves

88

· Being busy is a way of avoiding their problems and situation

· People admire their ability to multi-task, and this makes them feel good

· Time management becomes an issue and they might reach burnout, then they look for a Rescuer to save them

**Candy the Comfort-eater**

· Low self-esteem and often has poor coping skills

· Looks on food as a temporary fix when all else turns to custard

· Often feels that they have no control over their lives, and the only control they have is what they put into their mouths

· Will eat even if they are not hungry

· Usually non-confrontational and quite placid in nature

· Will often think of their eating as punishing those who hurt them, rather than punishing themselves

· Pattern could have started during an unhappy childhood

· May even hide away to eat or hide their food, but will tell you that they don't know why they are obese as they hardly eat anything

**Petra the Pathological Liar**

· Their lies fool a lot of people most of the time as they are so convincing

· They often believe their own lies, especially after they've repeated them enough

· Have difficulty differentiating between fact and fiction and sometimes don't even realise they are lying

- Quick thinking with a good memory makes them difficult to catch out
- Will often choose to lie rather than tell the truth, even if the truth isn't so bad at all

**Jack the Joker**
- Low self-esteem
- Often hides a deep sadness inside
- Is very social and has many acquaintances rather than friends
- Has a need to make people laugh and be the centre of attention
- Appears to never be serious about anything
- Subconsciously might worry about everything
- Always concerned about what people think of them

**Sylvia the Stalker**
- Very low self-esteem
- Often has suffered continued rejection in the past
- Creates a fantasy life with the other person in their mind, which is very real to them
- Has difficulty accepting that the other person doesn't want them or even know them
- They convince themselves that they'll be able to persuade their target to love them or want them
- Very obsessive, and can get very jealous of anybody else in their target's life
- Capable of harming themselves, their target, or people connected to their target if they feel their love is unrequited
- They focus so much on their target, that they don't have time for their day to day living, or developing new relationships

**Penny the Perfectionist**

·    If they have a low self-esteem, then they try and create an ordered, perfect environment, over which they have control

·    This could be a way to cover up disorder somewhere else in their lives

·    Disorder causes them anxiety and panic attacks

·    They could be obsessive compulsive people

·    They often choose partners who are the complete opposite to them, and use their desire for perfection as a way to control their partner

·    They get a kick out of other people complementing them on their perfection

**Martha the Martyr**

·    Very low self-esteem and self-image

·    Only way they feel worthy is by making sacrifices

·    When other people admire them or feel sorry for them for making sacrifices, then they feel good

·    Often end up being taken advantage of or being treated like a doormat

·    Soldiering on and being a Martyr is often a ploy to get rewards

·    Their favourite words are, "But look what I did/sacrificed for you..."

·    They appear selfless, but often have an ulterior motive

·    They often don't want to be rescued, as that stops them from being a Martyr and having a Pity Party

**Shawn the Scatologist**

·    Low self-esteem

- Judgmental and hyper-critical
- Will never take responsibility when they do something wrong
- They prefer to go back to all previous situations and altercations and sift through the brown smelly stuff, to throw in your face
  - They store past injustices to call upon, as a way of detracting from what they've done wrong
- They might occasionally forgive, but they never forget

**Pam the Pervert**
- Could have a low self-esteem
- Easily bored by the conventional
- Looks for different ways to get a sexual kick
- Has a desire to shock, thus grabbing the attention
- Could come from an abusive background
- Might be very conservative in their everyday lives
- Very curious, has a desire to experiment with new sensations
- Might be the only area in their life where they have some control
- Might be fearful of 'normal' relationships, because of being hurt in the past, and can become someone else by creating a fantasy situation, or prefer to watch as an outsider

**Nigel the Neglector**
- Is so involved in their own needs and interests, that they don't recognise the needs of others, especially their children
- Will withdraw from their family to meet needs outside their home

·   Has a very busy life, be it work-related, sport, hobby, drinking, drugs or even an affair so children left to fend for themselves
·   When they are at home, their mind is elsewhere, so children find them cold and rejecting
·   Often expects the older child to raise the younger ones and take care of their needs as well, and this causes an angry child who had to give up their childhood

We can also play Control Games.  Every time we help someone just so that they owe us; acquire power by any means; seek vengeance by punishing someone who has committed some grievous sin against us; tell lies and pretend to be nice; avoid a problem to get out of a hole; run away from things we think we can't deal with; take our problems at work out on our partner or continually make excuses for someone – allowing them to keep repeating their behaviour, then we are playing a Control Game.

**Autodysomophobia- Fear of one that has a vile odor.**

# CHAPTER 7
# I'm perfect, so why the hell must I change?

*Change yourself, and fortune will change with you.*
<u>Portuguese proverb</u>

Too often in life, we try to change our lives for the better by trying to change the people around us. We never think we are the problem, it's always the other person who is at fault. What we fail to realise is that for things to change, we have to change. If the other person has faults and problems, then it's their problem, not yours. They have to effect the change on themselves. Sometimes changing old habits is hard. There is no quick fix. You just have to make the conscious decision to change something about yourself you don't like – then do it! Maybe you think you're quite perfect the way you are, and there's no need for you to change anything about yourself at all. Well, the reality is, is that nobody's perfect. Ultimately, it's your choice whether or not you want to change. No partner, friend, counselor, person can force you to make changes. It has to come from within and be a desire you have, otherwise you won't have the motivation or willpower to do it. Most people need to change something in their lives – it could be the way they feel, their attitude, the way they act towards others or even how people treat them.

**Escaping from the Drama Triangle**

It's not easy to leave behind a lifetime of behaviours and game-playing. If you're dissatisfied with the game you're playing, then now is the time to make those changes and leave. Here are some **guidelines** for making that change:

·   You need to be aware of what role you are playing in the game. If you've got this far in the book, you'll have placed yourself somewhere in the Drama Triangle.

·   If you're not dissatisfied and quite happy being in the Triangle, then there's no real point to change, is there?

·   You have to conjure up in your mind an attractive vision for the future. The grass has to appear greener on the other side, for you to make the effort to cross the fence.

·   It doesn't matter which member of the Triangle changes first, or even if the others don't want to change. The decision to change is your decision, let them worry about themselves.

·   It isn't a good idea to just up and leave as there'll be unresolved issues and unfinished business hanging over your head, which could very well come back and bite you in the bum at a later date. This, of course, could affect your future life. However, if you feel you are in danger – then **GO**! You can deal with the unresolved issues at a later stage. Remember, for healing to take place, you have to forgive.

·   Before you say that magic word – **NO**, you need to have something else to say **YES** to. If you don't do this, then there is a very good chance you can slip back into the Drama Triangle. Also, be careful of caring supportive people who might come into your life at this point – they could just be Rescuers helping you into a new Triangle.

· Don't be overcome with guilt that you've ended up a member of the Drama Triangle. Most of us end up in there without realising it. It's like we're not fully conscious of what we're doing and temporarily lost control of our minds.

· If you just swap one role in the game for another, then you are not making a real change.

· You need to be aware of who the other people are in this game you're playing, and what roles they are currently in.

· Learn to love, respect and accept yourself. That way you can get in touch with blocked feelings.

· You need to learn to be direct and straight with people rather than playing games. They'll respect you more for that.

· Become aware of what the triggers are, all the hooks that might snare you and pull you back into the game. Notice what is happening but don't react to it.

· Stop blaming others, and start solving problems.

· Always strive to learn from your mistakes. It's okay to make mistakes as long as we learn from them.

· Try and surround yourself with positive people who have no need to play games.

· Set yourself clear boundaries and stick to enforcing the consequences should they be infringed on.

· Discontinue friendships with people who use and abuse you.

· Work hard on correcting your faults and weaknesses.

· Most importantly, forgive yourself, then move on.

· Become more honest by letting your outside behaviours match the feelings you have inside.

· Understand that the other members of your Triangle will now view you as the 'baddie ' when you refuse to play the old games.

· A Persecutor cannot force you to play Victim and vice versa – it's a choice you make.

· Sometimes we need to suffer the painful consequences of our choices and hit rock bottom, before we are ready to make a change.

**RESCUERS**

· Find other ways to make yourself feel good. Basing your self-esteem on helping others is not a good thing.

· Give up being a Superhero who flies in and helps the weak. You don't need to feel superior all the time because you are the good guy.

· Stop trying to control others. You don't always know what's best for them.

· Worry about yourself and your own problems and needs, rather than focusing on someone else's. Use your energy to solve your own.

· Learn how to recognise others' manipulation tricks and guilt laying techniques as hooks to drag you into rescuer mode again.

· Stop trying to justify your rescuing behaviour.

· Don't feel sorry for others who just want to use and abuse you. They don't feel sorry for you.

· Become assertive and learn to say **NO**, and then mean it.

· When victims overwhelm you with their problems, direct them where they can go for help, then leave them to sort out their own problems.

· Become responsible only for yourself.

**VICTIMS**

· Stop expecting others to always come and rescue you. Start standing up for yourself and taking responsibility for your actions and feelings.

· Start thinking and solving problems for yourself.

· Address your fears and work on building up your self-esteem.

· Learn how to deal with confrontation and anger.

· Learn how to set limits and boundaries and be prepared to enforce the consequences if they are crossed.

· Tape yourself when you go into victim mode and see what you can change to make yourself more assertive and more in control of your own life.

· Learn what triggers precede your collapse into helplessness and take steps to counteract them.

· When you hit a problem, get a blank piece of paper, imagine that you have a group of 50 experts sitting in a conference room just to advise you and you are their secretary writing down their advice. Now right down what you'd imagine they'd say.

**PERSECUTORS**

· Stop denying what you do to other people.

· Stop being overly critical.

· Give up on your desire to always be right and stop judging people.

· Stop trying to justify your behaviours and rather face up to the fact that your anger and unrealistic expectations seriously damage other people.

· Take anger management classes and learn how to control your anger.

· Address your fears, and don't try and hide away from them with your behaviour.

· Find other activities and pastimes to give you that adrenalin rush, rather than getting it from being angry.

· Learn other ways to feel good about yourself, rather than feeling good and powerful when you put others down or make them fear you.

· Respect other people's boundaries.

· Learn how to apologise to people you hurt, and really mean it.

· Work on repairing broken relationships between family and friends.

· Ask yourself the question, "What do I really want for myself?"

**When an abuser wants to change**

Are you terrified of not being in control? Terrified of having feelings? Terrified of rejection? Terrified of losing your partner? Do you need to always have control or power over the people in your life? Do you go to any extreme to preserve that power, even if it means hurting those closest to you? Are people terrified when you become angry? If you recognise these traits in you, then you could be slipping into the abuse trap. If you honestly want to change, then you need to do the following immediately – not tomorrow or next week – **NOW**!

1.  Take a good hard look at yourself. Do you like what you see? Do you see what effect your behaviours have on other people? Be honest with yourself.

2.  Read everything you can lay your hands on about abuse, and the effects of abuse. Being informed makes you more aware of what you're doing.

3.  Don't make assumptions about things, listen to your partner with an open accepting mind. It is okay to disagree. Life would be boring if we all agreed with everybody. If you disagree, just don't react with anger or withdrawal.

4.  Ask your partner to tell you every time they feel you do something abusive, or you cause them to feel fear. A good idea would be for them to write it down and discuss it with you at a later time, when you're not so uptight. You could have a set meeting time, when you and your partner have some quiet time to discuss these issues. A good technique is to sit next to each other with kneecaps touching. It's hard to get angry when you're sitting like that. Listen to your partner, and don't interrupt them when they speak. Another good trick is to write down the main points of what they're saying. This stops you from reacting in anger and helps you to take in what they're saying. When it's your turn to speak, you'll have a chance to justify your behaviour, or tell your partner what triggered off each set of abusive behaviour. This will help them to

understand you a bit better and to avoid the triggers. It's all about communication.

5.   Find out about the effects of abuse on families. Decide if this is the legacy you want to leave your children.

6.   Seek out the guidance and help from a trained counselor or therapist.  Don't try to do it all alone. You are trying to change a lifetime of bad behaviour patters, it's not easy and you'll need support from experienced people to bring about a radical change.

7.   Join a support group or anger management class. This might help you to work through personal issues in your life, root out the cause of your controlling behaviours, 'fly off the handle' anger and subconscious fears.

8.   Stop controlling everybody and everything.  Make a conscious effort to 'zip your lips' in situations that would previously escalate into something inflammatory.  You must want to change more than you want to control.

9.   It's an accepted fact that abused children often become abusive parents.  Decide today to make the decision to break the cycle of abuse.  What helps is if you say this affirmation out loud to yourself every morning.  So, you have just brushed your teeth, look at yourself in the bathroom mirror (nobody is watching you or listening to you so it's okay), and say out loud: "I am a good partner/parent.  I treat others with respect at all times.  I am able to control my anger and my mouth," Sounds crazy, but affirmations like that work.  Maybe it's to do with re-directing your thoughts, or engaging the power of the mind.

10. Make a conscious effort to make positive comments to your partner/children/family/friends/peers every day.  It could even be something very small like…."I liked the way you brought me a coffee when I got home from work.  Thanks, it was great."  I find so many people have nothing good to say about anything.  They see the worst in every situation and seem to delight in criticizing everything and pointing out all the bad points.  There is some good in everything.  Focus on the one good thing you see and rather make a comment about that.

11. What happens if you know what's best for your partner?  They have the right to make their own choices, including choices you may believe are wrong.  State your opinion once or twice then drop it.  Stop trying to control, guide or fix your partner.  Rather use that time and energy controlling yourself and learning to tolerate and accept your partner's choices.

A series of bad relationships can age you rapidly.

**Bogyphobia- Fear of bogeys or the bogeyman**.

# CHAPTER 8
## Fears, phobias and frozen feet

*He who fears to suffer, suffers from fear.*
<u>French Proverb</u>

"Crash!" Glass shatters somewhere in your house and you know that you are supposed to be alone at home. You feel the hairs stand up on the back of your neck, your feet seem to be frozen to the ground. "Fight or flight," is what goes through your mind. You feel your heart beating faster. Your mouth becomes dry. Your face has developed an ugly grimace. As you hear thuds in the next room, you feel a surge of adrenalin rush through your veins, and at that moment, you feel that you can annihilate any adversary. You reach for the bedside lamp…

Fear is nature's way of stopping us from getting hurt. When overcome by fear, your body goes into protection mode, releases all kinds of funny chemicals, shuts down different systems – all just to keep you safe from harm. Fears can range from a little scare, like when someone creeps up behind you when you are brushing your teeth – to paralysing terror and even passing out. Little fears can be quite exciting and give an adrenalin rush, like when you go bungy jumping. Extreme fears can make you irrational. When you can't think straight, you can be easily manipulated. Fear is the opposite of desire, and while desire attracts, fear repels. Pessimism leads to fear and fear can also come from confusion. New ideas can cause us fear. Even the bravest of the brave have experienced fear in their lives. Fear transcends all cultures, countries and continents. Even animals experience fear. Fear results in us doing one of two things – fight or flight.

When we have an intense fear of something, that we actually experience panic attacks and anxiety whenever we are confronted with it, then we can assume that we have a phobia. Usually if we know we have a phobia about something, then we avoid it like the plague. We might know that we are being silly and unreasonable, but we are just unable to overcome our fear. Although many phobias start out in childhood, they can actually impact at any age. I don't know if it's because men are supposed to be macho, or if they are just better at hiding their fears than women, but phobias are generally twice as common in women as in men.

Once we have identified that we have a phobia, it's not the end of the world. There are many ways to cure us of our phobias. First, we need to get educated about it, and read as much as we can lay our hands on. When we know what is happening to us and why it is happening, it will reduce the anxiety and we will no longer believe that our fear is going to kill us. The big thing, is to learn what triggers the panic attacks. Learning different relaxation techniques is also good. Sometimes, if we let one phobia control us and dictate our lives to us, then that might trigger another phobia and so on, until we're riddled with a whole bunch of phobias that'll turn our lives into a living hell. We then get to be more afraid of the panic attack than the actual phobia. So, if we take the situation, break it down into little parts and concentrate on overcoming each small part, eventually you'll be able to overcome the whole phobia.

An interesting form of therapy that can be used is called **Cognitive Therapy**. It was invented by Aaron T. Beck. Basically, it works on the premise that good and bad things happen to everybody – both happy and depressed people. It just depends on how you react. It's the half-full vs half-empty glass debate. Some people are able to see something positive in every situation. They have a major car accident and will react by saying something like, "At least we're alive and survived that!" or, "We needed a new car anyway so it's a good thing our car got written off." Then there are the people who see negative in everything, even when good things happen to them. A husband gives his wife a beautiful and very expensive watch for her birthday. Her reaction, "He's just trying to tell me I'm always late and never on time." Or, "He's a control freak, now he'll believe I don't have any excuse for doing things when he wants them done."

Having negative thoughts when good and bad things happen to us is just a bad habit. There's nothing medically wrong with you, you've just let yourself get away with it for years so that it's become ingrained into your psyche. Cognitive Therapy helps you to break those horrible old habits, by giving you techniques to help you find positive things you can rather say to yourself, and helps you to spot the negative thoughts and shut them out. Let's face it, having negative thoughts gives you a distorted picture of your life, and will help create more fears, phobias and anxiety. We don't want that, do we? So with Cognitive Therapy, you identify the thinking patterns that have corrupted your outlook on life. You change them and calm your mind so you feel better and voila! You are now able to think clearly and make better decisions, and not be so warped! And importantly, **no** drugs are used in this kind of therapy – it's all you and your therapist!

Many of our fears are unfounded or based on something that might have happened in our childhood. Either way, they have distorted our thoughts, which in turn has caused us to have negative feelings which has resulted in us showing undesirable behaviours.

So, if I was a mathematician, I would write something like this. **FEAR** is **DISTORTED THOUGHTS + NEGATIVE FEELINGS = UNDESIRABLE BEHAVIOURS**. When we are faced with our fear, we follow the same mathematical equation every time without fail. We don't check to see if there is any evidence to warrant our reaction. We just respond automatically, like we are on auto-pilot. It is a coping strategy that we devised for ourselves a long time ago. So, that explains why we might repeat the same kind of relationships over and over again, go for the same kind of people, react the same way when relationships go bad. It stands to reason then, if we change our distorted thoughts, we'll also change our negative feelings which will result in a halt to our undesirable behaviours, which would mean the end of our fear.

Many of us suffer from quite a few different fears, some of them overlap and others are as a result of other fears. For example, a *fear of commitment* could be because we have a *fear of rejection*, which is because we have a *fear of getting hurt*. It is very difficult to have a happy, successful relationship, when you have many deep-seated fears. And while no relationship is perfect and it is quite okay to have ups and downs, you do want to have happiness in your life – very difficult when we let our fears rule us and our relationships.

**Some common fears which could have an adverse effect on our relationships are:**

**Fear of Rejection** – *Your self-image is too closely tied to what people think of you. When you take responsibility for your own feelings of self-worth,* *instead of basing your self-worth on others' love and approval, then you can stop taking rejection personally.*

**Fear of Being Alone** – *You are so desperate not to be alone, so you hook up with the first person who shows an interest, often for the wrong reasons and very often the wrong person for you.*

**Fear of Failure** – *Nobody succeeds all the time, even apparently very successful people. It's the fear that hurts more than the actual failure. Failure is only a problem if we let it defeat us altogether and we don't even risk trying in case we fail.*

**Fear of Losing our Freedom or of Being Controlled** – *We are scared of not being able or allowed to do what we want, when we want. The fear often exists because we don't know how to handle the situation of being controlled, rather than from previous experiences. As soon as you learn to set boundaries and not allow others to invade, smother or dominate us, then we'll no longer fear losing ourselves in a relationship.*

**Fear of Intimacy** – *The actual fear here is of getting hurt or rejection. You can also be scared if you share too much of yourself with another, they'll take advantage of you, engulf you totally that you lose yourself.*

**Fear of Not Being Worthy** – *There is a car bumper sticker that says, "God don't make no junk." Remember that because it's true. If someone doesn't think you're worthy, that's their problem, not yours.*

**Fear of Trusting Someone Else** – *This goes down again to a fear of being hurt or let down. Someone hurt you in the past, so this is what happens every time. Don't generalise and give the other person a chance to prove themselves.*

**Fear of Not Being Attractive Enough** – *Remember that people who only base a relationship on looks alone are shallow and not worth knowing. When you actually bother to get to know someone and begin to like them, they become physically more attractive to you, regardless of how they looked to you at first.*

**Fear of Commitment** – *This goes down to our fear of rejection, getting hurt and losing our freedom.*

**Fear of Confrontation** – *We rather do anything else other than getting involved, so we feel bad later because we ignored our own needs or did something we regret.*

**Fear of Becoming Known as We Really Are** – *Sooner or later the true you will emerge, so why not share the true you with others at the outset, rather than waste all the time and effort building a relationship with someone who thinks they're involved with a different person.*

**Fear of Pain and Disappointment** – *Life is full of disappointments and there'll be many a time that you'll experience a sense of pain and loss. However, it is always balanced with a huge variety of good things. Focus on the good things you've experienced in life so far.*

**Fear of Being a Taker as well as a Giver** – *Some people only feel love when they are giving and are scared that if they take, they'll be viewed as selfish. Stop worrying about what others might think.*

**Fear of Judgment** – *People who judge others are usually covering up some undesirable qualities in themselves. They point out your mistakes to stop you from noticing theirs. It's their problem not yours. Get over it.*

**Fear of Showing Love and Affection** – *This goes down to a fear of intimacy, fear of hurt and rejection or simply they way you were brought up at home. If your parents were not demonstrative, it'll take a conscious effort on your part to learn to become demonstrative.*

**Fear of Being Loved** – *Once again the feeling of not being worthy and the possibility of rejection rears it's ugly head. Also, some people believe that if they let others love them, they lose their freedom and control over their lives.*

**Fear of Abandonment** – *This is usually based on past experiences. It's the actual fear, rather than the abandonment which is the frightening thing here. You survived before to tell the tale. Not everybody is the same and you might never get abandoned again.*

**Fear of Infidelity** – *This often causes men to avoid strong women as they perceive them more likely to attract other sexual partners. This is linked to our fear of rejection and trusting others.*

**3 Common coping strategies we use when faced with our fears**

**AVOIDANCE** which means we find ways to escape from or block out our fears.  We do this by:

· Withdrawing socially

· Focusing on independence and refusing to ask others for help

· Retreating into isolation by doing things which doesn't need another's presence like watching television, reading, surfing the internet, painting

· Throwing ourselves into shopping, gambling, sex

· Taking on addiction like drugs, alcohol, overeating, excessive masturbation

· Denying we have a problem

· Withdrawing into a fantasy world

**SURRENDERING** which means we just give in to our fears and end up repeating them over and over again.  This is a defeatist attitude.  We do this by:

· Relying on others to do everything and meet our needs

· Becoming clingy

· Becoming a people-pleaser

· Avoiding conflict at all costs

- Becoming submissive

- Always playing the Victim

**OVERCOMPENSATING** which means we do the opposite of what our fears make us feel. We do this by:

- Becoming hostile and aggressive by blaming others, becoming overly critical and abusive and also defiant.

- Becoming domineering and self-assertive

- Manipulating others

- 'Punishing' others by sulking, backstabbing, going out of your way to ruin things

- Attention seeking

- Trying to impress others by name-dropping or status-seeking

- Becoming a perfectionist and maintaining tight self-control and strict order

### Anxiety Disorders

Some people have problems mixing with others. They are paranoid that people are watching them and judging them, so they are afraid of going out and doing anything which might potentially embarrass or humiliate them in public. Often they might behave

112

strangely when faced with this phobia, and instead of blending into the background, will actually make themselves more noticeable. They'll show heightened anxiety by twitching, blushing, shaking, suddenly speaking with a croaky voice or breaking out in a cold sweat. Some people are so overcome with shyness, that they forget simple words and can't speak - well not anything that makes sense! Less noticeable symptoms might be developing a queasy stomach and having a desire to vomit, a dry mouth, tensing up all your muscles, dizziness, and the worst of all – when your heart starts thumping and it feels like it's beating in your ears or throat.

The over-riding fear these people have, is one of rejection. They tend to have a low opinion of themselves and only focus on the negative. Shyness is the most common anxiety disorder, and roughly 1 out of every 10 people suffer from it sometime in their life. Being shy and reserved is one thing, but acute shyness can have a negative impact on your life. People with this kind of social phobia are often single. Many drop out of school, live on welfare or battle to hold onto a job. They are often depressed loners who live on the brink of suicide. Others turn to drugs and alcohol for comfort. If you fall into this category, you need to seek help urgently.

Sometimes we might be under so much stress at home or at work, that we get panic attacks. These can happen at any time and nothing in particular sets them off. I can remember the first time I separated from Jason, I started getting panic attacks. My first one happened during a school assembly. To this day I don't know what triggered it off. I was standing next to my class, when suddenly I started hyperventilating – which made me so dizzy that I wanted to pass out. Then I could hear my heart beating in my ears, and feel it beating in my throat, and I struggled to breathe. The next stage for me was that I felt as if I was detached from myself. It was like I was watching the world as an observer, but nobody could see me. All in all, it was a very frightening experience, and one I've repeated a couple of times over the years. Sweating, clammy hands, trembling, chest pains, nausea, fear of losing control, fear of dying, numbness, pins and needles, cold shivers or hot flushes – are all other symptoms people might experience when having a panic attack. The best way to combat panic attacks, is to learn some relaxation techniques and also slow deep breathing.

Are you someone who worries about everything continuously? You don't feel as if you're functioning unless you have something to worry about? I seemed to spend my whole life worrying – about finances, housework, children and what the future holds. Now, I have been trying something new and it works. I just tell myself, "What's the point in worrying about something you can't change or do anything about." Worrying unnecessarily, is a waste of time and energy. Apparently there is a name for worry pots like us. It's called Generalised Anxiety Disorder, and more women suffer from it than men. If you suffer from this, you tend to struggle to have a good night's sleep so that you are edgy, irritable and very tired the next day. You'll also find you'll read the same page of the book over and over again as it impairs your concentration. I would imagine this would have a negative impact on your sex life as well. It's hard to lie back and think of England while you are trying to solve the worries of the world in your head. Jokes aside, it's treated the same as other phobias, and usually a sleeping tablet or two will do the trick.

After my cancer diagnosis and subsequent operation, I was treated for Post-Traumatic Stress Disorder. I couldn't sleep at night as I'd have recurring nightmares that someone would bump into me in the street, and my breast would fall off and land on the ground – lying there looking like a piece of rump steak. My breast surgeon thought it was hilarious and nearly fell off her chair laughing. But, my plastic surgeon wasn't amused and sent me to have therapy with the Cancer Society. Post Traumatic Stress Disorder is no laughing matter, and anybody at any age who has experienced some kind of trauma, could go through it. Families living in an abusive environment could suffer from it.

Basically, with this kind of stress disorder, you suffer from the same kind of symptoms as fears and phobias. Nightmares, which are often vivid re-enactments of the traumatic event, extreme distress when something triggers a memory, sweating, palpitations – are all unpleasant signs to look out for. Some people resort to avoidance – I couldn't bare to look at my scars or breast reconstruction, and used to cover up the mirror!  Yet others turn to drugs and alcohol to help them to forget about what happened to them.  Sometimes we block out the whole incident and it becomes a deeply buried memory.

The worst thing about Post Traumatic Stress Disorder for me, was the lack of interest in doing anything fun or being with other people.  I became completely apathetic and would go to the supermarket and feel that I was invisible.  I would go through the motions of grocery shopping, but it didn't feel like it was me doing it.  I went to a friend's 50th birthday party and spent the whole time in the kitchen preparing snacks, so that I wouldn't have to socialise.  For me that was really against the norm, as I am a very social person.  I felt permanently sad.  Nothing gave me joy and I was unable to make any plans for the future, as I didn't see a future for myself.  I was permanently tired, as I couldn't sleep at night, couldn't concentrate to read a book or watch television, and suffered from a serious sense of humour failure.  It was too much of a strain to even smile.  Although I was alive, I was only going through the motions of living, and then of course you get the well-meaning people who tell you to start smiling as you've beaten cancer and are lucky to be alive.  I didn't feel very lucky.  It felt like I carried the world on my shoulders.  I didn't know what was happening to me, other than I was fearful and couldn't cope with the simplest of tasks.

When my GP finally diagnosed me with Post Traumatic Stress Disorder, I felt a huge sense of relief. There was a reason for my strange behaviours. I read up all I could on the subject on the internet, and being informed gave me a deeper understanding of what was happening to me. The therapist I saw at the Cancer Society, taught me how to manage my depression, helped me work through issues and also taught me relaxation techniques. My GP put me on Prozac (but I stopped it after a month) and sleeping pills. A few good nights sleep were all I needed to get me over the worst of it. If you find yourself suffering from this disorder, I suggest you seek help. This is not something easily overcome by yourself.

There are many different treatments around. Some therapists believe in exposing their patients to a minor version of whatever fears them – until they become almost immune to it. Others believe in absolutely flooding them with whatever they are afraid of, until they are completely over-exposed with it, so that the fear reflex eventually fades away. Still others, train their patients to substitute some kind of a relaxation response for the fear response. The theory behind that, is that you can't feel scared if you're relaxed. Now, this is all well and fine if your phobia is spiders, but what happens if your real fear is your partner?

## Abusive relationships

When someone makes you afraid to be yourself, and afraid to control yourself so that you are available to be controlled by them, then you are a victim of abuse.

Outsiders don't understand what an abused person actually goes through. They tend to generalise, play down the situation and blame the Victim, by making comments like, "They must like being abused or they would leave."

"You are just a person who loves too much, so you brought it on yourself."

"You have a low self-esteem so you don't have the guts to leave."

"You did something to provoke the abuse."

"You over-exaggerate or make-up the abuse. It's really not as bad as you say."

"If your partner has a problem controlling their anger or stress, all you have to do is learn to keep out of their way."

"Abused people all come from poor, low class, uneducated backgrounds, so it's their lot in life."

The truth is, nobody enjoys being abused, be it verbally, physically or mentally, no matter what your self-esteem is like. People who are into sado-masochism are just playing games and what we might call abuse is just a part of that game. The difference in a sado-masochistic game, is that both partners are willing players. In an abusive relationship, one

118

partner is not a willing player, and is only staying in the game out of fear.

An interesting statistic, I don't know about abused men, but I read somewhere that 70% of domestic assaults occur after the woman tries to leave, and one-half of all battered women murdered, are murdered after they leave. So, don't judge someone who is staying in an abusive relationship. You don't know what fears are keeping them there.

**Top ten reasons we stay in bad relationships**
1.  **FEAR**
2.  **FEAR**
3.  **FEAR**
4.  **FEAR**
5.  **FEAR**
6.  **FEAR**
7.  **FEAR**
8.  **FEAR**
9.  **FEAR**
10. **FEAR**

Seriously though, it's all about fear. Fear rules us completely. So, if we know we're in a bad relationship, why don't we just leave? Well, here's **why we stay and hang on** by our short and curlies.
•   Fear you might put yourselves and your children in greater danger by leaving, you might have had threats
•   Fear of what leaving might do to the children emotionally

- Fear you won't be able to survive financially
- Fear of expensive court battles with lawyers and such like
- Fear of losing custody of your children
- Fear of downsizing your lifestyle and accommodation
- Fear of what family and friends will say
- Fear of the unknown – the grass may not be greener on the other side
- Fear to take the risk and make a huge life change
- Fear that you can't live without the abuse you've gotten used to over time
- Fear of upheaval and moving your children away from schools, friends, etc
- Fear of retaliation and reprisals – vengeance is mine sayeth the abuser
- Fear of not having enough time to plan the whole 'leave thing' properly
- Fear of loneliness
- Fear the abuser will commit suicide if you leave
- Fear that maybe you're just imagining how bad it is, and maybe it's not really that bad and other people have it worse
- Fear that nobody will ever love you or want you again
- Fear that the problems are actually all your fault
- Fear that your partner will change for the better after you leave

- Fear that your partner won't cope without you
- Fear that your family is not whole without a mother and a father
- Fear that you're going against your religious beliefs – till death us do part….and all that
- Fear that you just don't have the necessary energy to leave
- Fear that you might not have the support to get you through this tough time
- Fear that you don't have the skills or training to get yourself a good job
- Fear that maybe you're a bad person and don't deserve better anyway

To be able to conquer our fears, we need to know what they are. Once we've identified our fears, we need to be aware of what might happen to us should our fears be realised. Sometimes, what we think might happen to us, is all in our minds, and in reality - it would never turn out that way or be as bad as we imagined. Writing it all down helps to bring us back to reality.

## MY WORST FEARS, BOTH REAL AND IMAGINED

| FEAR | HOW DOES THAT MAKE ME FEEL? | WHAT DO I THINK WILL HAPPEN TO ME? | WHAT EVIDENCE IS THERE TO SUPPORT MY THOUGHTS? |
|------|------|------|------|
|      |      |      |      |
|      |      |      |      |
|      |      |      |      |
|      |      |      |      |
|      |      |      |      |
|      |      |      |      |
|      |      |      |      |
|      |      |      |      |
|      |      |      |      |

If you plan on running
from everything - make
sure you wear the
correct clothing.

**Catagelophobia- Fear of being ridiculed.**

# CHAPTER 9
## Panic Mechanic

Sometimes we try so hard to change our environment, using every possible method but never succeeding, that eventually we come to expect to fail. The constant resistance to our efforts to change things, causes us to feel helpless and puts us into panic mode. The best way to avoid panic setting in, is to set clear boundaries and let everybody know your limits.

**Setting boundaries to avoid panic**

Boundaries are invisible lines drawn to distinguish areas where your personal responsibility begins and ends. Only you have control over your boundaries. It's important to point out that no boundary is cast in stone or set in concrete – unless you choose to make it that way. Abusers and co-dependents are known to have weak boundaries. They lack self-control, but we were born with free choice. We are in the position we are in because of choices we've made in the past. We made the choice to let someone cross our boundaries, and in doing that, we've lost control, lost our freedom of choice, lost our self.

We are responsible for everything about ourselves – for our feelings, values, behaviours, dreams, goals, thoughts, choices, insights, beliefs, and – you guessed it – boundaries. If you keep on letting people trespass, and keep on resetting your boundaries to suit them, then you are turning yourself into a doormat and that is your responsibility. You are allowing yourself to go into panic mode. It is easier to keep the sheep out of the paddock when the fence is fixed and the gate closed, rather than trying to get them out and then mend the fence and close the gate.

Throughout my marriage, I constantly reset my boundaries and moved my limits to avoid confrontation.    I was scared of the consequences of saying 'no'.  This made Jason constantly try and cross my boundaries.  It became a kind of challenge to him.  I felt guilty when I set limits.  He made me feel guilty when I set limits.  But, I realised that ultimately, I was responsible for my feelings, and Jason was responsible for his feelings and actions.  It isn't your responsibility to make your partner happy or miserable.  Your responsibility is to yourself.  For years we get taught that being selfish is a bad thing.  Maybe, we need to think of another word to use instead of 'selfish', one that doesn't have such a bad connotation.  But, looking after yourself by setting boundaries, is a good thing.

When I first moved in with Jason and realised he had an anger management problem, I set a very important limit.  I said to him, "If you ever raise your hand to me, don't ever go to sleep."  Now that might sound a bit dramatic, but I meant it.  I don't know what I planned to do when I said that, maybe hit him over the head with a cast iron frying pan while he was asleep, I don't know.  However, that was one boundary that was cast in concrete.  It took him quite a few years to cross that boundary.  He probably thought he'd get away with it as I'd let him cross all my other boundaries. The day he lifted a hand to me, punched me on the jaw and then tried to strangle me in front of all his staff at his work, I drove straight to the police station and laid a charge of assault against him. He couldn't understand how someone who supposedly loved him could do something so mean to him, as to give him a criminal record. A missionary friend of mine said at the time, "He has to learn that what he did was unacceptable behaviour."

Jason must have had a short memory, as a couple of years later when he was in a severe depression and decided he wanted to kill us all, he beat our then 3 year old daughter black and blue as she was full and didn't want to finish the sandwich he'd made her. When I got home from work, I whisked her straight up to the police station, only to be told that as he hadn't killed her, it was too much paperwork to open a case. However, as the bruising from the beating was quite bad, they recommended that I get a restraining order against him. This I did, and when he broke it the very next week, he was locked up and that finally (thank God) signaled the end of our 10 year relationship.

When I set a limit and stuck to it, I had such a feeling of power. It took away my panic, my fear of him and he never frightened me again. The amazing thing, was that he must have picked up on my new sense of power, as on the few occasions I saw him afterwards, he was no longer the bully but a simpering wimp. People who abuse others do so because the Victim hasn't set clear boundaries. It's like you teach your children – for every action, there's a consequence. If they do the action, then they have to experience the consequence, otherwise they'll just keep on doing it. Set your boundaries and stick to them. Don't stick to them one day and let things go the next. You have to be consistent, otherwise you're going to let panic enter again.

It's human nature to build up feelings of resentment against people who continuously cross your boundaries. How could you ever feel good about yourself when you're weighed down by all that baggage?

I once had a boss who was a bit of a control freak. He was very short and very fat, but would make snide comments about other fat people. His girlfriend was the director of the company, and she was very tall and thin. He told her how ugly she was and how unprofessional she looked (which she didn't) and made her change her style of dress, make-up, hair colour, hairstyle and even her make of car! She did whatever he told her to, to please him. He said that he had felt embarrassed when he went with her to meet clients before, as he could only feel good about himself, if his friends and clients were impressed with her. She couldn't recognise her limits and stick to them, so she lost all her power. In a staff meeting, in front of everybody, the boss told the office manager she looked like an old frump and needed a new look. Needless to say, he had buttons missing from his shirt and food stains down the front of it! When I arrived at the office and saw the office manager sporting a new hair colour, hairstyle, dressed like a clone of the director - all because my boss had told her she looked like an ugly duckling…I thought it was a good time to leave that environment. The office manager had let him cross her limits. When he said what he said in that staff meeting, she sat there with a fixed smile on her face, but inside she was in a panic. She fled the building straight after the meeting, straight to the director's favourite hair salon.    She needed to say, "I'm happy with me and the way I look.  If you don't like the way I look, it's your problem, not mine.  Get over it!"

We can't change who we are because someone else tells us who we should be.  This works both ways.  We can't force our partners to change to fit the mould we want.  It's their personal choice to make those changes.  Too many relationships end up on the rocks because of one partner trying to make the other partner fit the mould they designed.

As your boundaries develop, other people's boundaries no longer matter.  A friend had a very attractive and vivacious wife.  He was very insecure and used to get jealous if other men admired her.  He set boundaries that were related to his jealousy.  She was only allowed to drive his flashy car if he was with her.  It didn't matter if he wasn't using it and it was just standing there.  He didn't want other men to look at her when they were drawn to the car.  He was setting limits to try and control her, and the poor woman couldn't understand why she wasn't good enough to drive his car without him!

It is definitely a worthwhile exercise to take some time to work out exactly what your boundaries are. How can you enforce them, if you don't even know what they are yourself? It is also important to work out the consequences if someone crosses your boundaries. If you have worked out in advance what the consequences are, then it is easier to be consistent when you dish out your 'punishment' every time you stick to your boundaries.

| BOUNDARIES I WANT TO SET IN CONCRETE | CONSEQUENCES IF SOMEONE TRIES TO CROSS MY BOUNDARIES |
|---|---|
|  |  |
|  |  |
|  |  |
|  |  |
|  |  |
|  |  |
|  |  |
|  |  |

Part of setting boundaries, is listing the qualities you want and don't want in a partner. In doing this, you set boundaries or limits for yourself. If you take the time to sit down and work out exactly the type of partner you are looking for, then you might avoid the trap of grabbing onto the first person that comes along because you're lonely and don't want to be alone. All too often, our fear of loneliness causes us to grab hold of the wrong person for us. We then condemn ourselves to a miserable relationship for who knows how many years.

I have a friend who married the first person who showed an interest in him. His marriage was very rocky, with occasional separations, a little bit of infidelity, and many full blown fights and spats. To avoid the ongoing confrontation, he retreated into his own little world. Their marriage is more peaceful now, because after more than 20 years, he has resigned himself to the fact that this is his lot in life and they have become more tolerant of each other.

## QUALITIES I'D LIKE IN MY IDEAL PARTNER

|  |
| --- |
|  |
|  |
|  |
|  |

## QUALITIES I DON'T LIKE IN A PARTNER

|  |
| --- |
|  |
|  |
|  |
|  |

**Defecaloesiophobia- Fear of painful bowel
movements**

# CHAPTER 10
## The Blame Game

*Adam must have an Eve, to blame for his own faults.*
German Proverb

*Blame is the lazy man's wages.*
Danish Proverb

People who blame others have perfected the art of 'scapegoating'. Deep inside they believe that they are above reproach and they will lash out at anybody who criticises them and they'll sacrifice whoever or whatever who tries to dent their self-image. They might tell you that they only did it for your own good, or they were trying to help or save you from yourself. The worst part, is that they get indignant when you don't show proper thanks for what they did.

Blame is just a defense mechanism. The pain each person feels is real to them, and it's often very painful to take responsibility for something that goes wrong or doesn't work out. The only way out of playing the Blame Game, is to change your thinking and start taking responsibility for your actions, accept your past and learn to forgive others. It's no good holding onto past hurts and using them as convenient excuses from time to time.

It is completely normal for someone with lots of fears, to believe that everything they feel is somebody else's fault. We don't want to take responsibility for our own fears. The Blame Game really gets into a higher gear, when each partner starts blaming the other for everything wrong in their lives. Their relationship becomes like a war zone, with each one sniping at the other. "I had a bad childhood, so I can't help the way I am. If you were more understanding about that, then you wouldn't force me to behave badly!"

That often results in the other partner sniping back, "Your bad behaviour has caused me to feel badly about myself and to think I'm worthless. Therefore, I'm too scared to think for myself and that's your fault!" Of course in reality, the language they use might not be as savory as the language I used. Regardless of that, you cannot win in the Blame Game. Resentment, fear, anxiety, loss of self-esteem, anger – are all by-products of this game.

People who rush into rebound relationships after a break-up, are also playing the Blame Game. This isn't really fair on the new partner who is usually an innocent Victim in the Game. Rebound relationships are just the hurt partner's way of saying, "I wasn't at fault for the break-up. Look, someone else wants me now. I am lovable and desirable after all, so the fact the relationship didn't work out has got to be all your fault!"

That's the beauty of always blaming others, we just blame everything bad that happens on someone else. That way we stay perfect because it's never our fault. My youngest daughter is already a good player of this Game. A good example, and one that seems to happen quite often, is her bringing me a mug of coffee she made for me. My son, as usual, will be clowning around in the room. She'll look at him and spill some coffee on the floor. Immediately, before anybody can even say anything, she'll start shouting at him for making her spill the coffee. How did he do that? He was on the other side of the room at the time! My daughter'll tell you, that he made her look at him, so therefore her spilling the coffee is solely his fault. She's very clever. If she does something wrong, she'll always react immediately with anger at all and sundry. She gets in first with the angry outburst, blaming others at the top of her voice, and that serves to take the attention away from what she did wrong. Unfortunately for her, we are all on to her, so she doesn't get away with the Game she's playing. Hopefully, she'll eventually realise her strategy doesn't work and will start accepting the responsibility for the things she does. At the moment though, her Blame Game is all about – 'Look what you made me do!'

Other people are just as cunning, if not more. Steve used to push my friend Angela's buttons, until she couldn't take it anymore, so she would react emotionally, often with a huge outburst. His instigating, button-pushing and winding her up would be so subtle, that other people around her wouldn't notice it. They would, however, notice Angela's reaction, and they would sympathise with Steve for having such an 'out-of-control' wife. Steve would then have an excuse to physically 'restrain' Angela, as he was 'worried' she might harm herself. The sad thing, was that everybody agreed that the bruises Angela got every time Steve had to restrain her, was her fault. Even a therapist they saw, said that as long as Steve's actions continued to arise out of good intentions, then it was okay! Steve managed to blame Angela for his bad behaviour, and he's still getting away with it!

You have to remember, that people abuse or use you because there is something wrong with them. You haven't done or said anything wrong – the problem lies with them. Basically, they have a low self-esteem. They don't like themselves, and rather than trying to change what they don't like, they make others take the responsibility for their behaviour when they lay the blame on them. Deep down, they know you don't deserve it, so they hate themselves all the more for hurting you, so it's all your fault that you make them hate themselves – it's just a vicious cycle they can't seem to break. Eventually over a period of time, they actually start believing it is all your fault, because that makes them feel as if they haven't done anything wrong. You can't try and explain things to them, or lay a guilt trip on them. In their eyes, they have done no wrong, so you are just wasting your breath.

Often, we blame others for holding us back. We might say, "If it weren't for you …" or "If I didn't have children, I would…" We use other people as a convenient excuse to avoid doing something. It's easier to just give up, avoid taking that risk or making that decision, and putting the blame squarely on someone else.

A great example of this is Jason. (The poor man must surely be feeling his ears burning by now.) I can remember Jason wanting to buy a Mercedes Benz. As

136

I was the only one bringing in an income, I told him we couldn't afford it and had no need for it. Our Volkswagen was just fine for our family. Jason refused to accept the fact that we just could not afford a Mercedes. He tried many strategies to persuade me to let him trade in my Volkswagen for that Mercedes. First, he would introduce the fact that he just 'happened to drive past the car yard and the Mercedes was still there – unsold, must be a sign' into every conversation. When that didn't pique my interest, I would have to hear how they let him take it for a test drive and it had the quietest motor ever. He went on and on about the Mercedes, and what a great deal they offered him on it. I stayed firm and held on to my "No, we can't afford it." When these tactics failed, the Blame Game started in all seriousness.

"You don't want me to succeed in my life. You don't want me to have anything better than you. You always have to be the best. You have to always be in control and the only successful member of the family. I could have been somebody if it wasn't for you always holding me back to make you look good!" This was often accompanied by temper tantrums and things been thrown around and a helluva lot of swearing. At me naturally, because I was the bad person here. I took all of that blame and abuse, because I knew that we just could not afford that car.

His next attack, was that the reason he couldn't sell any offshore investments and get commission so he could contribute to the family table, was because he didn't drive a car befitting a successful businessman. His logic was, that if he drove around in a Mercedes, then people would see that he was successful, so then they would do business with him. Therefore, it was my fault that he didn't contribute to the family income, as I wouldn't let him drive a car befitting a successful businessman.

Then he changed tack. He told me that he hadn't wanted to alarm me, or cause me worry, but the cylinder head in the Volkswagen had a huge crack in it, and he was expecting the engine to seize or the car to conk out and give up the ghost at any time. Not being a Petrolhead, I didn't know what to look for in the engine to see whether or not he was telling the truth. I suspected that his story was all bullshit, but by this time I was so tired and exasperated with the whole car saga, that like a dumb mug, I gave him the benefit of the doubt and….yes. I relented.

Jason never explained the details of the great deal he had organised, to me and I stupidly assumed it was just the normal kind of Hire Purchase deal he had arranged. Well, what eventually came out, was that he used my Volkswagen as a deposit, and told them that he was a high earner and would pay 10 000 the one month and 15 000 the next. Just for the record, I was only earning 2 500 a month at the time! Needless to say, he never paid them a cent bar the initial deposit with my car as trade-in, and they repossessed the Mercedes the third month that he had it. My Volkswagen that was used as a deposit was lost in the deal that never was, and we were completely carless. The final straw, was when Jason turned to me after they took the car away, and said, "This is all your fault. If you had had the balls to stand up to me and say no, then this wouldn't have happened!"

I have to say, that sometimes I think you can't win. It's like – you're damned if you do and you're damned if you don't. As you can well imagine, this little incident wasn't very good for our marriage at all. Things got worse when I came home with a car I bought from a tax refund. Jason's reaction was the classic, "Well what can I say? You are a better man than I'll ever be!"

Serial Cheaters thrive on playing the Blame Game. It gives them a reason to do what they're doing, so it gets them 'off the hook'. Because you do realise, that they'll believe that what they're doing is never their fault. They don't get enough sex or attention at home, so they are 'forced' to go out elsewhere and find it. It's not their fault they are forced to cheat! So the moral of the story is, don't kill yourself trying to make someone happy who keeps finding ways to lay all the blame on you when they cheat. The same as, if you decide to stay with them and keep giving them chance after chance, then that is a choice you've made, and you can't one day turn around and blame anyone for the choices you made. How often do you hear from friends, "I only stayed with him/her for the sake of the children." What utter bullshit! How dare you blame the children, for you staying in a loveless unhappy relationship! You only stay in that relationship, because you are too scared to leave for whatever reason. The children are just an excuse, because reality shows that children adapt easily and are far happier in a loving happy home, than a home with unconcealed anger and resentment bouncing off the walls in every room. Children are not stupid just because they are young. No matter how hard their parents might try to disguise and hide their relationship problems, children always sense when things aren't right and are very aware of what is going on.

Cheaters are quite predictable, because if they have done it more than once in the past, they'll continue to do it in the future. Don't ignore it and just hope that things will work out. Be honest, tell them what you don't like and if they aren't prepared to fix it, then you have to decide if you can live with it or not. If living with it makes you desperately unhappy, then move on. Remember, fix the problem and not the blame.

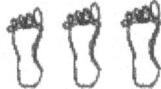

Martin was devastated when he came home early one day, and found Cathy in bed with another man. He felt no less devastated, when he caught her a second time and then a third. Cathy blamed him for her infidelities. It was his fault because he was often too tired to pay her the attention she needed because he worked so hard. Martin started watching Cathy like a hawk, coming home at odd times, phoning to check she was home and alone. Cathy started accusing Martin of being a control-freak and would lose her rag and stomp out of the room when he questioned her about her activities. She told Martin he was being paranoid whenever he asked her if she still saw other men. Eventually, Cathy started getting aggressive and would pick up objects and throw them at Martin, or throw them at windows and break them. Martin started getting nervous and stopped asking Cathy questions, as he was scared of upsetting her and putting her in an aggressive mood. He started to believe that he was guilty of wrecking the relationship. Months of constantly being told his paranoia and being overly sensitive was going to push her into relationships with other men if he didn't drop it, finally took their toll. Martin ended the relationship.

Martin realised that he fell in love with an idea – a fantasy that was backed up by things Cathy had promised initially. When Cathy's actions contradicted his fantasy, he would start questioning her and that would lead to both parties playing the Blame Game. Paranoia and blame became the pattern of their relationship. Martin missed what he wanted to have in the relationship – the idea, his fantasy – what he kept hanging in there for and never had. Now, Martin has problems dealing with the demise of their relationship, because Cathy never took responsibility for her actions, and always put the blame for everything solely on Martin's shoulders.

It's amazing how constant blame can eat into our self-esteem, until we actually believe that we are responsible. Recognise blame for what it is and stop taking responsibility for others' actions. When you stick to your guns and keep to your limits, you can be accused of being vindictive. So what? That is their problem, not yours.

**Dishabiliophobia- Fear of undressing in front of someone.**

# CHAPTER 11
## Moving from pain to gain

*For one pleasure a thousand pains*.
French Proverb

How many times in my life haven't I heard my mother say to me, "Don't let it get you down, look on it as something that makes you stronger." I can remember many a time throwing my hands up in the air and crying out beseechingly, "How strong do I have to be? Bloody Atlas carrying the world on my shoulders!" Unfortunately, my mother was right. Each adversity, each trial, each test we face does strengthen us, and with each one we grow a little more. Whether we manage to move from pain to gain depends solely on us.

Some people like to dwell in the pain area for a while. They play the Victim, evoke the sympathy, get the attention, and feel very sorry for themselves. I suppose they feel that they have gone through hell, so they deserve to lap up attention and sympathy for a while. However, sooner or later there has to be a cut off point, a point where you say, "No more feeling sorry for myself." A point where you are ready to move on and face a new set of adventures life has for you. Everybody is unique, so everybody's cut off point will be different. What was good for you, isn't necessary good for someone else. Staying too long in the Pain Zone isn't very healthy though. You can become depressed, overcome with fears of all shapes and descriptions, and lose all your self-esteem. That of course, will bring you a whole new set of problems.

The biggest hurdle preventing people from moving on after a failed relationship, is **LOVE**. When one partner calls it quits and leaves the relationship, it doesn't mean that the other partner automatically stops loving them the moment they walk out the door. They can still love the other person, even though they have been left behind. To be in love alone is one of the hardest kinds of love to have. It is heart-wrenching stuff, and if it happens to you, you'll keep on analysing and re-analysing every little incident to see what you could have done differently, and how you could have prevented your partner from leaving. You will probably blame yourself for all that happened or went wrong. Well, initially, that is what you'll do, and then you'll probably change to the "Vengeance is mine!" stage. The more you loved your partner, the more hurt and pain you feel, the bigger the revenge you'll seek. Sounds horrible and a little dramatic, but it's true.

You are very vulnerable at this stage of your life, and this is when many so-called 'reconciliations' occur. The partner that left might suddenly realise that the grass isn't greener on the other side, or their new partner has dumped them and they want to go somewhere safe to lick their wounds. They know that you still love them (Crikey! You've kept telling them that over and over again since they left, how could they not know), and they will feel safe and secure with you. Of course you forget all your planned acts of revenge and take them back with open, loving arms.

Initially the relationship will be good, but unfortunately, 9 times out of 10, after a couple of months, you're back where you started. Hurt, depressed, overcome with pain and fear. How do I know this? Well, it's happened to me more than once. It's happened to quite a few people I know. It's a pattern that we have to break. There is always the chance that you could be the 1 out of 10 reconciliation that makes it. However, I strongly believe that for that to happen, all issues that caused the initial break-up have to be completely resolved. What tends to happen, is that we are so happy to have the 'love of our life' back, and we are so grateful not to have to face our future alone, that we pack all the issues into the old kitbag and keep them in storage for later use. To hang on to the 'loved one' we might even let them cross our boundaries, just to keep them happy.

To move out of the Pain Zone, we have to change our attitude. Our self-esteem is in tatters, we are feeling worthless and unloved. A good way to start feeling better about yourself, is to write down the best compliments you've ever received. Even though we are constantly told not to worry about the approval of others, it is natural and quite normal to seek other's approval and use that as a yardstick for ourselves.

| MY TOP 10 COMPLIMENTS I'VE EVER RECEIVED |
| --- |
| |
| |
| |
| |
| |
| |
| |
| |
| |
| |

## Self-affirmations

These are positive thoughts we use to counter our negative thoughts. They make us feel good about ourselves and give our lives a positive direction to work towards  Very importantly, they help us to take personal responsibility and stop depending on others for approval, as well as giving us permission to grow. Self-affirmations help us to let go of negative baggage we carry around in our kitbags, and helps us to move away from people who drain our life-juice out of us.

Think of those people as 'emotional vampires'. When you start to visualise, imagine or believe in your success prophecies, they do start to come true. It's a case of feel it, believe it – and it's yours!

I found that the best way to counter any negative thoughts, was to write my affirmations down and read them every morning when I woke up, and every night just before I went to sleep. It's almost like, putting on your suit of armour to protect you from the bombardment of negative thoughts other people will hurl at you all day. And then at night, it gives you something to focus on in your dreams. It definitely keeps nightmares and polar bears away! You have to make sure that the affirmation you write down is positive – can be; might be; I think; can possibly be – all have no place in an affirmation. You have to be quite clear in your statement. Short statements are better, as you can recite them to yourself during the day if things get rough. Don't worry about people thinking you're crazy if you're talking to yourself! That's their problem, not yours!

So, if you have a new date on the horizon, the first one after your relationship ended, you could be nervous and quite anxious. It's not easy going back into the dating game after many years out of it. Don't let yourself drown in your fears. Write out a set of affirmations to prepare yourself for the date.

1. *I am attractive.*
2. *I am confident.*
3. *I am pleasant company.*
4. *I am a very interesting and entertaining person.*
5. *I am very likeable.*

146

Read them twice a day, believe them with all your heart and when the date comes, you'll ooze confidence and wow the date off their feet.

Maybe you are wanting a new car or a new job, or even a new relationship. Write down positive affirmations.

*I will get a new car.*
*I will get the right job for me.*
*I will start a relationship with the best partner ever.*

It's amazing, but when you start to become more positive you start sending out positive signals, and positive things start happening to you.
Write down some positive self-affirmations for yourself. Remember to read them every morning and every night, and in fact, any time you feel down.

| MY SELF-AFFIRMATIONS |
| --- |
| |
| |
| |
| |

**Euphobia- Fear of hearing good news.**

# CHAPTER 12
## Mirror, mirror on the wall

*"You must be the change you wish to see in the world."*
Mahatma Gandhi

Always remember, what you put out to the world is what you get back. If you believe you are a worthless piece of 'no good dog doo', and act accordingly. Then, that is how people will treat you. If you like to always portray yourself as a Victim, then you'll always attract Rescuers. If you treat everybody around you with mistrust and suspicion, then they'll cheat on you and let you down. It's like, people have a subconscious desire to live up to your expectations. So, if your expectations are low, that's what you're going to attract back. Human predators only attack or take advantage of those they think won't fight back. Someone is only going to use you as a doormat if you project that you are prepared to let them wipe their dirty feet on you.

If you act that you are self-confident and have a good, healthy self-esteem, then what you'll get back is people treating you with respect. If you keep acting as if you are overflowing with confidence, sooner or later you'll start believing it yourself and then you will be self-confident. It's a simple theory, is very true and it works!

Simon was hurt when Jenny dumped him. She did it in such a cruel way, that he actually became terrified of women. Before, he used to look for caring, kindness and compassion in women. These were qualities he wanted. However, after being publically dumped in a busy restaurant, he started looking for different qualities in women. He looked for signs of bitchiness, cruelty and insensitivity. As a result, he only attracted women with those qualities to him, and as soon as they showed them, he ran away. Not literally of course. What Simon was putting out, he was getting back. Now he thinks all women must be like that as he never seems to find women with any of the good qualities he once wanted. What he doesn't realise, is that he is no longer looking for women with those good qualities. He is focusing all his attention on the bad qualities, and that is what he is finding and getting back. Think of all the really nice women out there now being overlooked by him. They might be attracted to Simon, but are too scared to approach him, as they think that he is only attracted to bitches!

What you need to do now, is think about what you are putting out to all and sundry. What are other people seeing when they look at you? If you are constantly being trampled on, abused, taken advantage of or treated with disrespect, then have a good look to see what exactly you are portraying out there. Look at each area of your life and think of at least one thing you can change.

## CHANGES I WANT TO MAKE IN ME AS A PERSON
## EMOTIONS/ATTITUDE/SELF-ESTEEM

|  |
| --- |
|  |
|  |
|  |
|  |

## CHANGES I WANT TO MAKE IN MY CAREER

|  |
| --- |
|  |
|  |
|  |
|  |

## CHANGES I WANT TO MAKE IN MY HEALTH

| |
| --- |
| |
| |
| |
| |
| |

## CHANGES I WANT TO MAKE IN MY FINANCES

| |
| --- |
| |
| |
| |
| |
| |

| CHANGES I WANT TO MAKE IN MY IMAGE |
|---|
| |
| |
| |
| |
| |

| CHANGES I WANT TO MAKE IN MY RELATIONSHIPS |
|---|
| |
| |
| |
| |
| |

| CHANGES I WANT TO MAKE IN MY EVERYDAY LIVING |
|---|
| |
| |
| |
| |
| |

**Helminthophobia- Fear of being infested with worms.**

# CHAPTER 13
## One small step…

*It does not matter how slowly you*
*go so long as you do not stop.*
<u>Confucius</u>

Changing a whole lifetime of negative thought
processes is not something you can just do overnight.
It's not like you go to sleep one person and wake up
the exact opposite of the person you were the night
before. Change takes commitment, self-discipline,
time, energy and hard work. It's far easier to break
down what you want to change into small bite-size
chunks with achievable goals. That way, every time
you achieve a small goal, you get spurred on to
achieve the next, and so on. This helps to keep us
motivated. There's nothing worse than setting
yourself a big goal, and getting disillusioned as no
matter what you do, you don't seem to get any closer
to reaching it.

How many overweight people try a new diet, set
themselves a goal to lose 20kg in 6 weeks, and then
give up after the second week? The goal they're
setting themselves is out of reach – a surefire path to
failure! It doesn't matter how old we are, we still
like to be rewarded for our efforts, and to experience
that sense of accomplishment whenever we reach a
target. So, if you want to lose weight – the big goal
is 20kg, but you break it down into an achievable

weight loss each week, then reward yourself by treating yourself with something – maybe not a chocolate, then you'll feel good about yourself and try harder the following week.

When Sir Edmund Hillary decided to climb Mount Everest, he didn't just wake up one morning, say to himself, "Today I shall climb that ruddy mountain and achieve what no man has achieved before me." And then half an hour later look down on everybody from the top of the world. His Mount Everest expedition took a lot of planning, everything would have been broken down into small steps. First this has to be done, once done then the next stage will be planned and so on. All of this would have taken time and not been an overnight thing.

So to with the changes you make in your life. It doesn't matter how small the step is, as long as if it's in the right direction, you are making progress. There will be times when we are forced to take two steps back. When that happens, you need to start moving forward again, one step at a time. Don't be tempted to miss out steps, as they invariably come back to haunt us.

Think about back-up plans and coping strategies you can use to continue your advance. Edmund Hillary would have thought about back-up plans in case things went wrong.

## WHEN FACED WITH THE POSSIBILITY OF SOMETHING UNPLEASANT

| WHAT'S THE WORST THAT CAN HAPPEN? |
| --- |
| |
| |
| |
| |

Now, think of some coping strategies you could put in place and back up plans you could make to help you get through the unpleasant situation, should the 'worst case scenario' materialise.

| MY BACK UP PLANS |
| --- |
|  |
|  |
|  |
|  |
|  |
|  |
|  |
|  |
|  |

It's important to achieve a balance in our lives, therefore it's a really good idea to motivate yourself by working out what's the best that can happen should this unpleasant situation eventuate. Often, what really happens, is something in between the worst case scenario and the best case scenario.

| WHAT'S THE BEST THAT CAN HAPPEN? |
|---|
| |
| |
| |
| |

Sometimes, when we are so depressed, anxious or totally overcome by our fears, we can't think straight. Just doing the normal everyday tasks we do in our everyday living becomes too hard for us and too much to cope with. We then retreat into our self and start avoiding everything. This halts our progress, and stops us from moving towards our goals. If you find that this happens to you, then you need to break the small steps down into even smaller steps, making it easier to achieve and easier to cope.

My stepdad used to be addicted to making lists. He had lists for everything, lists of books he had to read and in what order, lists of what he needed to buy the next time he went to the shops, lists for jobs he needed to do around the house. We used to make fun of his lists, but looking back, he always had everything under control and was ready for any emergency that might crop up. If he didn't have his lists, he would become quite anxious and stressed, and we knew then to keep out of his way. What my stepdad was doing, was organising his life into small steps that were easily manageable.

Now, we don't have to take it to the extreme that he did, but getting a diary and working out an activity plan for each day is really worth doing. It helps you to cope better, and gives your day some sort of structure. You especially need this if you are wallowing in depression. Being surrounded by chaos, helps keep your mind in a chaotic state and you lose control of everything – both your environment and your mind. Small steps help you regain that control.

So, get a diary, and write down all the things you need to do each day. Make sure you have something that is potentially pleasurable, an activity that you can complete and give you a sense of accomplishment and something that will involve another person. Tick off each activity as you complete it. If you find an activity too hard, break it down into smaller steps. Tick off each step as you do it. Regaining control of your life will bring you closer to achieving your goals.

## Rubbish Bin Approach
Another good way to get rid of negative thoughts, is to use the Rubbish Bin Approach. Write down

something you don't like or a negative thought you are having, and throw it away in the rubbish bin. This is quite cathartic, and really works, clearing your mind from those nasty negative thoughts. You really need to get rid of negative thoughts, as hanging onto them causes:

- *Feelings of anger or resentment*
- *Feelings of guilt*
- *Feelings of failure*
- *Feelings of jealousy*
- *Feelings of inferiority*
- *Feelings of shame*
- *Feelings of being stressed out*
- *An overdependence on others' approval*
- *Lack of self-esteem*
- *You to stop taking risks*
- *You to believe that you are a loser*
- *You to only see doom and gloom for the future*
- *You to create a barrier of cynicism*
- *You to build the Great Wall of China around yourself*
- *You to become depressed*
- *You to create strong feelings of self-pity*
- *You to work subconsciously to fulfill the prophecy*

**Remember that positive thoughts counter negative thoughts.**

**Ithyphallophobia- Fear of seeing, thinking about or having an erect penis**

# CHAPTER 14
## What's holding you back?

While there are many reasons we might not get started on change, the most common reason that holds us back is procrastination. When we procrastinate, we put off doing something till the next day, then the next day and so on. We convince ourselves, I'll start on that goal once I've done this....and then when the time comes to start, we'll think of something else we have to do first, until we completely forget about our desire to change.

Procrastination is supposed to make our lives more pleasant, but instead causes us great stress. Because all the time, in the back of your mind, the thought that you have to eventually do it, is hovering.

Procrastination makes us disorganised and gives us a sense of failure, as it hinders success. It's just an escape route from fear - fear of facing reality, fear of life's challenges, fear of hard work and fear of leaving your comfort zone.

**What is hope?**

Hope happens when someone sees something and decides that that's what they really want, and although they are realistic enough to believe they might not get it, they believe that there is always a chance they will get it. So if you have hope, then what can be holding you back? The answer is **FEAR**. Fear is negative hope.

There are 3 kinds of hope.  Hope can range from virtual certainty to utter desperation.  The first kind is **DESPERATION**.  Think of refugees trying to escape from their war-torn country.  They have that desperate kind of hope, where they feel a deep need to escape and they'll do almost anything to get away– be it trusting untrustworthy people, stealing, lying, hiding in a shipping container and facing possible suffocation, swimming in shark-infested waters, taking to the open sea in a crowded leaky unseaworthy boat.  Desperation causes us to take chances we normally wouldn't dream of taking.  I remember when we were trying to flee from Jason as he had broken a restraining order and told the neighbour across the road how he was going to kill us.  I stupidly trusted my next door neighbour when deep down I knew that she was pulling a con on us.  But, we were so desperate to get away, I let myself be taken in by her lies and that ended up in us being destitute and homeless 1500km away, and her rifling through all our possessions (for which she'd organised storage), and selling off anything of value which we had.  It was a hard lesson to learn.  Desperate hope doesn't always end well.

**OPTIMISM** is when you hope against all hopes that it will happen.  You often have some evidence that it will, but you do realise that there is still a small chance of failure.  **REALISTIC HOPE** is when there is over a 50% chance of it happening.  Many people are just happy to hope,  however, if you dash their hopes and are perceived as the culprit – be prepared for possibly becoming the target of their revenge!

Hope-stealers also hold you back. These people get pleasure in putting you off your dreams, goals and desire to change. They are very negative people and only see the negative in every situation. Basically, they are completely ruled by their fears, so they don't want to see you succeed. They want you to give-up as that makes them feel okay and not inferior. If you ignore them and achieve your goals, they feel bitter because you have 'shown them up'. They steal your hope, your desire to improve yourself, belittle your efforts – just constantly put you down. And they do all of this – wait…this is the good part…they do all of this in 'your best interests'. Avoid such people. If they start trying to steal your hope, interrupt them and say, "Thank you for your input, I'm sure you mean well, but I've decided to give this a go after all." They won't like that at all. Some might try and stab you in the back, or go out of their way to ensure that you fail. Just remember, that that is their problem, not yours. You are better than them. Don't let them distract you and take your eyes off your goals and your dream. That is what they want. Don't let them succeed. Don't give them the opportunity to say their favourite words, "I told you so." You can use their negativity as your motivation to succeed.

**Barriers to change**
1.  Flat out denial that you have a problem.
2.  You make excuses all the time and are reluctant to admit you have a problem.
3.  You start rebelling against other people who try and force you to change.
4.  You believe that you can't do anything about your problem, so you resign yourself to the fact that you'll stay the same.
5.  You believe that someone else is responsible for your problems and you are the Victim, so therefore the onus is on them to fix the problem.
6.  You start rationalising the problem in your mind, so that it doesn't seem so bad after all, and in doing that, you can avoid having to change.

So, the question is, **how on earth do we change those big burly barriers into stepping stones to success?**

- We need to become honest with ourselves, and admit that we are just making excuses to avoid changing.
- We need to face reality and rather find good reasons rather than excuses, to persuade ourselves to change. If we do this, then we can enlarge the gap between who we are now and who we can become if we change. If you have a big gap between the two, your motivation will be all the bigger.
- We need to become committed to change, because if we make a half-arsed attempt, we'll give up at the first hurdle.
- We need to avoid friends who 'support' you by telling you that you don't need to change as you're 'ok' the way you are.
- We need to remember not to only focus on the *pros* of changing, but to think about the *cons* as well. Changing a behaviour means you replace it with something else. People who give up smoking often have a great weight gain as they replace it with perpetual snacking or chewing lollies. Make sure you think about what you'll be replacing a changed behaviour with.
- Recognise and accept that you have weaknesses, but don't try to hide behind them and offer them up as excuses.
- We need to understand what is important for us and not somebody else. We are making the necessary changes to achieve our goals and not someone else's goals.

- Try and achieve a balance by not letting your weaknesses dominate your strengths.

Our thoughts are often distorted, and they can be what's holding us back. Distorted thoughts can cause us to over-react in certain situations. So that, while we are committed to change and taking a step forward in the right direction, something happens, our thoughts are distorted so we over-react, and we end up taking 3 steps back. If this happens quite often, we'll give up as we don't feel that we're making much headway. The best way to solve this problem, is to analyse our thoughts. How did we react? How would someone else have reacted in this situation? Are my thoughts justified? When you take a closer look, you'll be amazed and it'll put the whole scenario into perspective.

**WHEN I OVER-REACT ABOUT SOMETHING**

**What was I doing at the time?**

**How did I feel?**

**What thoughts went through my mind?**

166

Remember, there is no 'quick fix'. You are not going to change overnight. You can't rely on other people to help you to change. This is something you have to do yourself. You can ask them for advice and support, but the actual change has to be done by you. We are all unique and therefore we all have our own agendas and effect the changes in our own time. Don't let other 'well-meaning' people try and dictate to you how long the change process must take. You'll do it in your own time, when you are ready. You are the Master of your own Destiny. Take back control of your life.

**Macrophobia- Fear of long waits.**

# CHAPTER 15
## B.Pos isn't just a blood group

My blood group is B.Positive and somehow, by luck or chance or divine intervention, it has always been the motto I have used throughout my life. It is natural to be overcome with depression and anxiety when something bad happens to you. However, too many of us get caught up in the whole 'anxiety', and get stressed out as we let our fears take over. What we need to do, is take a step back and try and focus on something positive that we can take out of the bad situation. Once we do that, we can work on changing negatives into positives.

I am the eternal optimist. Jason had his doctorate in Negative Thinking. Even when things went well, he'd look for bad things to complain about, and get anxious about. Of course, when you start searching for bad things, they won't let you down – they'll appear. Jason had the amazing ability to bring doom and gloom into a room full of happy people. This happened on many occasions, we'd be at a party or function. Everybody would be chatting and laughing happily. Jason would walk in, and without him saying a word, conversations would stop, happy laughter and chatter would end, and when conversations started up again, there would be a subdued tone to it. Don't ask me how this happened, Jason wouldn't say a word, so it would be nothing he said which caused it. Somehow or other, his presence just seemed to create it. Over the years, quite a few friends of mine remarked on it, saying that he just seemed to permeate doom and gloom when he walked into a room. Like it was a bad aura he gave off.

For a long time, I believed that my eternal optimism would brush off on Jason, and help him change into a more positive person, a person other people would want to have around. In time, I realised that I would never change him. The only person who could change him was him, and he wasn't prepared to change at all. He enjoyed wallowing in his misery and having people feel sorry for him. Those who tolerated his presence that is.

Having a positive attitude on life is something only you can develop within your self. Nobody can put it there for you. I have faced many adversities in my life, and I'm grateful that my positive attitude carried me through them and helped me to overcome them. When a bad situation arises, I'll get depressed or anxious initially. My fears will surface, I might have a panic attack or two, I'll focus on the worst case scenario. That might make me feel really down, but then I start thinking about Plan A, Plan B and Plan C as ways to cope with the situation. Then I'll start thinking about the best case scenario and will start feeling positive and good about everything. I'll know that I have already devised coping strategies if the bad things happen, and once you have Plan A, B and C in place, it doesn't seem so bad. Nine times out of ten, what ends up happening is something in between the worst case scenario and the best case scenario.

If you are feeling very negative and have a desire to change your attitude to a positive one. You need to start focusing on what makes you happy, rather than

what causes you fear, anxiety, anger and misery.  So,
if a negative thought enters your mind, replace it with
a thought of something that makes you happy.

| I FEEL MOST HAPPY WHEN… |
| --- |
|  |
|  |
|  |
|  |
|  |

Write down what makes you feel happy so that you
commit it to your mind and don't forget it.  Often
when we have the tendency to always focus on the
negative, we forget that there are times when we do
experience happiness.  Being happy helps us to
develop a positive attitude.  Rehashing good memories
also works to overcome negative thoughts.

| MY TOP 10 BEST MEMORIES |
| --- |
|  |
|  |
|  |
|  |
|  |
|  |
|  |
|  |
|  |
|  |

**Metathesiophobia- Fear of changes.**

# CHAPTER 16
## Goals are Gaols

*The man who has no imagination has no wings.*
Muhammad Ali

It's amazing how many people ridicule people who have dreams. However, if there were no dreamers, we wouldn't have the modern technology we have today. Dreams are important and limitless. They provide us with a vision for the future and the direction we have to to take. Dreams inspire us, give us hope and help us to make decisions on how we want to live our lives. Dreams are all about our perfect purpose for being on this planet anyway. Do you dare to dream? Many of us don't as we're too scared. We let society and what other people think, limit us. We don't want to be thought of as fools, so we stifle our dreams and bury them somewhere deep inside us.

I always dreamed of being a writer one day, but so many people tried to put me off by telling me how one can't get published, raising their eyebrows or just dismissing my dream out of hand. So, I buried my dream, every now and then it would resurface, but other people always managed to bury it again with their negative comments. Now, I am not trying to blame others for me burying my dreams, it was I who buried it – not them. I was so concerned with what other people thought of me and their opinions, that I buried myself along with my dreams. Sometimes, it takes something life-threatening like a brush with

Cancer, to make you forget about what other people think, and be prepared to follow your dreams.

There is a popular misconception you have to change in your mind. Dreams are not goals. They are not the same thing at all. Goals grow out of dreams. In fact, goals are what get you your dreams.

| MY DREAMS (DON'T PUT LIMITS ON YOUR DREAMS) |
| --- |
| |
| |
| |
| |
| |
| |
| |
| |
| |
| |
| |

Sometimes, we get so focused on our goals, that we lose sight of our dreams. Our goal is to lose 2kg in a week. We do it and it's like – wow, I succeeded. Now, let me reward myself with that huge slice of passion fruit cheesecake I saw in that Café…It shouldn't end when you succeed and achieve a goal, but often that is where we end it. We can't see beyond the goal post. Now, I'm not dismissing goals here, what I'm trying to say, is don't let them restrict you in your thinking. Look on goals as small steps towards achieving your dreams. Don't get so caught up in your goals, that you let your dream vanish into Never-Never Land somewhere.

Goals help us to achieve more, they can improve our performance, they can even enhance our motivation, they create pride and satisfaction in our accomplishments. They can completely eliminate self-defeating attitudes and our desire to 'give-up' when the going gets tough, With all of this, you will also find a huge improvement in your self-confidence which will in turn, raise your self-esteem. Goals are mega-important as they can be life-changing. If you fear change, leave it in my piggy-bank. Jokes aside, as goal setting is so important, you need to be able to set goals properly. Try and start off with one goal in each area of your life.

**Guidelines for Goal Setting**
·  Make sure the goal you are working for is something you really want, and not just something that sounds good and will impress others.

· Set goals in each area of your life to maintain balance.  I don't want you to go all lop-sided on me!

· Make sure the goals you set are consistent with your values.

· Make sure your goal is high enough but still realistic.  Easy goals make us lose interest.  Unrealistic goals make us give up.

· Write down your goals in complete detail, focusing on the positive – what you want, not on the negative – what you want to leave behind.  The more information we can feed into our subconscious minds, the easier it will be able to process it.  So, the clearer the final outcome will become.

· Don't be tempted to share your goals with others.  It's human nature to be 'supportive' by pointing out all the pit-falls and telling you stories how other people tried and failed.  They'll just discourage you and make you give-up.

· Think about all the things that can stand in your way and stop you from achieving your goals.  Think of ways that you will counteract the hurdles.

· Think about what steps need to be taken and what else you'll need to help you achieve your goal.

· Visualise your goal.  Close your eyes and see what it'll be like when you've achieved it.

· Read through your goals when you wake up in the morning, and again before you go to bed.  This must be done on a daily basis.

· Whenever you are faced with a decision, and don't know what to do – ask yourself, "If I do this, will it bring me closer or further away from a goal."  If it's going to take you further away, you know what your decision must be.

· Stay focused.

| MY HEALTH GOAL IN DETAIL |
| --- |
|  |
|  |
|  |
|  |
|  |

| MY CAREER GOAL IN DETAIL |
| --- |
|  |
|  |
|  |
|  |
|  |

| MY IMAGE GOAL IN DETAIL |
|---|
|  |
|  |
|  |
|  |
|  |

| MY RELATIONSHIPS GOAL IN DETAIL |
|---|
|  |
|  |
|  |
|  |
|  |

| MY FINANCES GOAL IN DETAIL |
| --- |
| |
| |
| |
| |
| |

| MY PERSONAL GROWTH/EMOTIONS/ATTITUDE GOAL IN DETAIL |
| --- |
| |
| |
| |
| |
| |

| MY GOALS | OBS. THAT CAN STOP OR SLOW ME DOWN | WAYS I CAN OVER COME THE OBS. | DATE I'D LIKE THIS GOAL ACHIEVE BY | WHAT I NEED TO HELP ME ACHIEVE THIS GOAL | POSITIVE RESULTS/BY-PRODUCTS OF ME ACHIEVING THIS GOAL |
|---|---|---|---|---|---|
|  |  |  |  |  |  |
|  |  |  |  |  |  |
|  |  |  |  |  |  |
|  |  |  |  |  |  |
|  |  |  |  |  |  |
|  |  |  |  |  |  |
|  |  |  |  |  |  |
|  |  |  |  |  |  |
|  |  |  |  |  |  |
|  |  |  |  |  |  |
|  |  |  |  |  |  |
|  |  |  |  |  |  |

You've written down your dreams, set your goals, you're on your way!  Remember not to let reality kill off the possibilities of your dreams.  Reality limits you, so you only bring in reality when you start strategising and setting your goals.

It's okay to give up on dreams that no longer suit you, fulfill you or make you happy.  It's pointless hanging onto a dream that makes you miserable.  Get rid of old dreams.  It's rather like a grocery cupboard. You can't find room to pack away your new groceries if the cupboard is jam-packed full of old groceries that are half-eaten or you decided you don't like.  Clean out the clutter and make room for your new dreams.

## **Good Luck!**

**Panophobia or Pantophobia- Fear of everything.**